I Garden: Urban Style

(Far Left) Photo by Anya Khait. (Middle) Photo by Ric Deliantoni. (Near Left) Photo by Catherine Macdonald.

I Garden: Urban Style

by Reggie Solomon and Michael Nolan

BETTERWAY HOME

CINCINNATI, OHIO
WWW.BETTERWAYBOOKS.COM

I Garden: Urban Style Copyright © 2010 by Reggie Solomon. Manufactured in China. All rights reserved. No part of this book may be reproduced in any form or by any electronic or mechanical means including information storage and retrieval systems without permission in writing from the publisher, except by a reviewer who may quote brief passages in a review. The content of this book has been thoroughly reviewed for accuracy. However, the author and publisher disclaim any liability for any damages, losses, or injuries that may result from the use or misuse of any product or information presented herein. It is the purchaser's responsibility to read and follow all instructions and warnings on all product labels. Published by Betterway Home Books, an imprint of F+W Media, Inc., 4700 East Galbraith Road, Cincinnati, Ohio, 45236. (800) 289-0963. First Edition.

 Other fine Betterway Home Books are available from your local bookstore, online, or direct from the publisher. Visit our website, www.fwmedia.com.

14 13 12 11 10   5 4 3 2 1

Distributed in Canada by Fraser Direct
100 Armstrong Avenue, Georgetown, Ontario, Canada L7G 5S4, Tel: (905) 877-4411
Distributed in the U.K. and Europe by F+W Media International
Brunel House, Newton Abbot, Devon, TQ12 4PU, England, Tel: (+44) 1626 323200,
Fax: (+44) 1626 323319, E-mail: postmaster@davidandcharles.co.uk
Distributed in Australia by Capricorn Link
P.O. Box 704, S. Windsor NSW, 2756 Australia, Tel: (02) 4577-3555

Library of Congress Cataloging in Publication Data
Solomon, Reggie, 1975-
  I garden : urban style / by Reggie Solomon and Michael Nolan. -- 1st ed.
      p. cm.
  Includes index.
  ISBN 978-1-4403-0556-6 (pbk. : alk. paper)
  1. Urban gardening. 2. Urban gardens. I. Nolan, Michael, 1972- II. Title.
  SB453.S615 2011
  635.091732--dc22
                        2010027189

Urban Garden Casual is a trademark of Reggie Solomon.
Edited by Jacqueline Musser; designed by Clare Finney; production coordinated by Mark Griffin

On the cover: (Top right) Photo by Steven H. Miller. (Bottom left) Photo by Frances Kuffel. (Bottom center) Photo by Kevin C. Matteson. (Bottom right) Photo by Regina Grosby.

Thank you to the following people and organizations for allowing F+W Media to photograph their gardens: Kate Cook, Dave Schwinn, Over-the-Rhine Homegrown, The Civic Garden Center's The People's Garden, Bryn Mooth.

About the Authors

Reggie Solomon

Reggie Solomon is the creator of two blogs—
UrbanGardenCasual.com and TomatoCasual.com. Urban
Garden Casual is focused on helping urban dwellers garden, and Tomato Casual is focused on everything tomato
for people who love tomatoes. When he is not hanging
out downtown, enjoying seasonally appropriate wines and
dancing with friends, Reggie enjoys tending to a small
backyard garden located a block from the intersection of
I-95 and I-91 in New Haven, Connecticut, where he grows
more than twenty varieties of tomatoes and ten varieties
of basil.

Michael Nolan

Michael Nolan has been a gardener since childhood and
is the founder of the Riverside Community Garden in
Atlanta, Georgia. He is a full-time writer who lives the
casual gardening lifestyle that he writes about. Michael
also hosts the weekly Internet-based radio show "The
Cheap & Easy Show" that combines gardening and frugal
living topics with the music of unsigned musicians from
all over the world, bringing a lighthearted and comic
appeal to what were once considered boring pursuits.

Dedication

To Michael Jackson
*Man, I miss you so much. Your music will groove
in my heart forever.*

To my mama, daddy, sister and paw-paw
(Thelma, Elbert and Leigh Ann Solomon and
Purvis Posey)
I love you.

–Reggie Solomon

I would like to dedicate this labor of love to my grandparents, *R. E. "Pete" and Mary Lee Combs and C.T. and
Nell Whisonant,* who taught me that the only tools
necessary to be a successful gardener are equal parts
love, respect, determination, and patience. It is my hope
that those lessons live on through this book.

–Michael Nolan

Acknowledgments

This book would not have been possible without the rock-
star writing power of Michael Nolan, a long-time member
of the Urban Garden Casual writing team. Michael, thank
you so much for helping birth this book with me.

I also want to thank the other members of my Urban
Garden Casual and Tomato Casual writing teams (yeah,
we dig tomatoes, too) for all of their many contributions
in helping build our "casual" gardening community and
this book: Vanessa Richins, Michelle Fabio, Cindy Naas,
Kira Hamman, Danny Thompson, Amy Jeanroy, Mindy
McIntosh-Shetter, and David Harbilas.

Lastly, thanks to the following special people who
have all been part of my gardening and personal success:
Kam Lasater (HB#1), J.R. Logan (HB#2), Meg Graustein,
Christine Kim, Claudia Merson, Michael Morand, Frank
Mitchell, Janna Wagner, Johannes Enders (love ya, baby),
Adriaan "Adii" Pienaar, and the cities of New Haven and
Montreal (whose cuisines and culture I simply adore).

–Reggie Solomon

contents

(Left) Photo by Katie Aaberg.

Preface

We are going to help you become a more successful urban gardener—*yeah, for real.*

Google lists UrbanGardenCasual.com, the website on which this book is based, within the first three search results whenever anyone searches for info on urban gardening, so we're definitely recognized for knowing our stuff. In fact, whip out your iPhone right now, type in "urban garden," and see for yourself. How do you think our publisher found us?

We created this book to make it easier for you to garden in the city in a casual style that fits your busy life and schedule. Join us for a journey through the world of *gardening done urban* and *gardening done casual.*

–Reggie Solomon

On March 23, 2008, I began a professional relationship with someone who shared my odd love for the tomato. That was the day I first began writing with Reggie Solomon on the website UrbanGardenCasual.com and its sister site, TomatoCasual.com. It didn't take long for the two of us to become friends, and his is a friendship that I have treasured ever since that day. I dare say that without that bond, this book may never have seen the light of day.

Whether you are a brown-thumb beginner or a seasoned pro, we hope that *I Garden: Urban Style* will soon become one of the most referenced books in your arsenal. While Reg and I couldn't possibly be more different, our love for gardening and for tackling the challenges that lie in the modern urban gardening environment have helped us create what we think is one of the best books on the subject in existence today. From asparagus to zinnias, we've got you covered, and though challenges will no doubt arise, you'll be prepared for whatever comes your way.

This book would not have been possible without the efforts of Casual team contributors Vanessa Richins and Michelle Fabio who each have a passion for gardening that is simultaneously admirable and frightening. To them and to the many wonderful readers we have met along the way, I say a sincere and heartfelt thanks for making this casual journey so worthwhile. It has been said that I was born with my hands in the dirt, and be that as it may, I hope that when my time on this beautiful planet is up, I'll go with dirt under my fingernails and a fresh heirloom tomato on my tongue.

–Michael Nolan

1 The Urban Garden Casual Philosophy

Although it is true that life in the city is loaded with perks, it has never been known for being particularly friendly to those who enjoy the simpler pleasures of tending their own gardens. By creating a marriage between the time-honored techniques employed in the traditional garden and the space and time challenges that are ever-present in the urban gardening environment, the Urban Garden Casual philosophy was born as a way to give due respect to both. Finally, a fun, healthy and money-saving hobby could be brought to a new generation of unlikely gardeners! For *I Garden: Urban Style*, we have drawn on the philosophy that has been at the very core of UrbanGardenCasual.com, the website upon which the concept of this book was built, since the site's inception in 2007.

So what is this Urban Garden Casual philosophy? First and foremost, this casual approach to gardening was designed with a *can do!* attitude that means anyone, anywhere can use these ideas and concepts, whether you have been gardening for years or you can't keep a houseplant alive. No matter where

Author Spotlight: Michael Nolan

I'm the oddball cousin you never want to introduce your friends to, mainly because you can never be too sure of what might come out of my mouth. You might say that I am the least-serious "serious urban gardener" you will ever meet.

All joking aside, I have been gardening nearly all of my life; the only thing that has changed over the years has been the venue. From huge plots on my grandparents' farm in Alabama to a few containers on my terrace in New York City, I have always found a way to grow my favorite vegetables and herbs no matter where I happened to be at the time.

By the time I founded a community garden in Atlanta in 2009, I had been gardening for more than a quarter of a century (*for those trying to do the math, that's twenty-five years*). Though I love all vegetables and fruits, I admit to having a special place in my heart for heirloom tomatoes. I have been collecting and growing heirloom seeds for years, and yet not a single year goes by that I don't find another one to try.

you are with regard to your experience, this book has advice that will help you.

Life is tough enough as it is; we don't need to leave our stressful jobs only to go home and carry that stress around for the rest of the day. Stress affects our lives individually as well as the lives of our loved ones. It can also affect our health. There has never been a better time to understand and embrace the Urban Garden Casual philosophy of gardening made urban and gardening made casual. Not only will you learn a hobby that can put food on your table or beautify your home, you can lower your blood pressure and get a little exercise to boot. What more incentive could you need to get out of your 9-to-5 clothes, grab your iPod and get casual?

When limited space, light, and the unique microclimates that are created by tight clusters of tall buildings all seem to be working against you, all you need to do is adopt the casual philosophy and you will arm yourself with the knowledge you need to get the best possible results from your efforts and your investment. Whether you are starting from scratch on a cramped fire escape or stretching your gardening wings into a plot at your local community garden, you will find the inspiration, motivation, and education you need to get started right.

There has never been a better time to understand and embrace the Urban Garden Casual philosophy of gardening made urban and gardening made casual.

(Above) Photo by Julia Claire Jackson, Neal's Yard, London.

Why Garden?

In order to make sure everyone starts on a level playing field, we are going to assume that if you bought this book, you likely have little to no experience with gardening. If you have gardening experience and you still bought this book, bless your heart!

Much like so many college theater majors, we are going to take a good look at motivation. Why should you garden? The answer can be as simple or as complex as you allow it to be. Maybe you need to save some cash. Growing your own food is one of the easiest and most cost-effective ways to do it.

(Above) Photo by Reggie Solomon.

The Urban Garden Casual Philosophy is about reclaiming the peace, relaxation, and satisfaction that comes from growing something yourself.

Reason #1: Cost

Cost is a huge factor when deciding to plant vegetables and fruits in your urban garden. While doing some quick shopping over lunch the other day, I saw heirloom tomatoes being sold at a popular whole-food retailer for $6.99 a pound! A fellow shopper looked at the sign and sucked her teeth in disgust. "I don't guess we'll be having fresh tomatoes tonight," she mumbled. I couldn't stifle a bit of a chuckle.

Why did I laugh at such a ridiculous price? Simple. I knew I'd be going home that afternoon and picking pound after pound of my own fresh heirloom tomatoes from the mammoth plants next to my garage, and those wouldn't cost me a penny.

Don't misunderstand—I wasn't laughing at the woman's plight; I was sympathizing with it whole-heartedly. I have seen it happen too many times over the years; during seasons when I didn't grow a garden (yeah, there were a few of those), I have been the one turning my nose up in disgust not only at the cost of fresh produce, but also at the pathetic quality we have become used to in our supermarkets. That brings me to the next reason.

Reason #2: Quality

Not only does homegrown produce cost less, but the quality is undeniably better than what you are likely to find in any produce aisle. After you have experienced what real, fresh, homegrown vegetables taste like, you may never be able to buy a tomato or cucumber at the store again. That freshness and obvious improvement in appearance and taste carries a noted increase in health benefits as well.

Reason #3: Health and Safety

If you grow something yourself, then you and only you are responsible for what goes into it, right? That means if you want real organic heirloom tomatoes that don't cost $6.99 a pound, you can start them from seed and know without any doubt that the tomatoes in your summer salads, salsas, and sauces are as organic as they could possibly be. Even if you aren't particularly sold on the whole organic thing—and we're risking sounding a little alarmist here—how do you really know what was in the fertilizers

Author Spotlight: Reggie Solomon

(Right) Photo by Reggie Solomon.

Perhaps I should have been a farmer. My mother and father are both from farming families in Mississippi, where farming was not just *a* way of life, it was *the* way of life. I can still remember the treat of chewing fresh sugar cane grown on my grandfather's farm as a small boy—a pleasure I still connect with today whenever I'm served a frozen sugar cane stick with a summer mojito.

Urban gardening is my modern farming legacy. I may still grow grapes and make wine one day.

In rural Georgia, where I grew up, I always kept a backyard garden, but eventually lost touch with gardening during college, graduate school and my early working years. Fortunately, I reconnected with my love of gardening, but this time in the city—New Haven, Connecticut, to be exact—where I work for my alma mater, Yale University. I have to admit that gardening in my urban backyard that borders the downtown and is one block away from the intersection of two interstate highways is a wee bit different from rural gardening.

and pesticides used to grow the mass-produced stuff you're getting at the supermarket?

In essence, the Urban Garden Casual philosophy is about reclaiming the peace, relaxation, and satisfaction that comes from growing something yourself. Whether it be a bouquet of beautiful flowers or a basket full of fresh produce, it is important to have that small diversion from an otherwise hectic life in the urban environment to help keep us grounded.

Gardening that Fits Your Schedule

From TomatoCasual.com

We all know the urban lifestyle is busy. You may be wondering if you have enough time for this new endeavor. If you follow the Urban Garden Casual philosophy, you will.

Timothy Ferriss's book, *The 4-Hour Workweek,* contains principles that can help you streamline your work life. We believe these same principles can be applied to cultivating an urban garden.

To start, we need to remember the simple formula Ferriss sets out

for anyone seeking to build a successful business or life: the key principles of Definition, Elimination, Automation, and Liberation, or **DEAL**.

Definition. The first part of success lies in defining what you want from your garden. While the idea in Ferriss's book applies to determining how much you want to earn in a given year, quarter or month, we will apply it to a growing season and how much you hope to grow during that season. Do you want enough tomatoes for fresh use in salads, salsa, and sauces, or do you want to give some

away to family and friends? Do you want to try your hand at canning?

Get a pen and paper and write down your expectations. Take a realistic look at what you would like to accomplish with your tomatoes this season and plan your plants accordingly. Will you need determinates, indeterminates (see chapter 5), or both? You will also need to plan your schedule for watering and fertilizing.

Elimination. In his book, Ferriss explains how he has used the Elimination principle to establish an information

(Left) Photo by Ed Cormany.

diet and only check his e-mail once a week. The point is to eliminate the unnecessary time-wasters in order to spend your time doing the things you love. To apply that to gardening, you want to look for ways to eliminate the more tedious chores in your urban garden.

You don't have to eliminate everything, especially those things that you particularly enjoy. The point here is to simply eliminate any unnecessary steps.

In chapter 5, we discuss companion planting as a means to help your tomato plants grow better with fewer pests and to produce tastier fruit. Companion planting also can eliminate at least some of the need for fertilizers and pest control.

Likewise, the act of growing the tomatoes in the first place eliminates the need to spend as much money at the supermarket.

Automation. After you have eliminated all of the unnecessary processes, the next step is to automate all of the remaining tasks that you possibly can. In our tomato garden example, this might mean adding nematodes as a preemptive strike against certain pests or adding a soaker hose around the base of your plants to make the process of watering that much quicker and easier.

You might consider moving containers closer to the path you are most likely to travel to reduce the number of steps required to pick the tomatoes when they are ripe. If you can harvest the fruit as you walk in the door from the porch, the process becomes automatic by default.

Liberation. The whole message behind *The 4-Hour Workweek* is to maximize the enjoyment we are getting out of life while minimizing the stress and time we spend doing things we don't enjoy or care about. When you use this method, you are in essence liberating yourself from those things you don't want or need and improving the quality of your life as a result. This isn't streamlining for the sake of streamlining, but for the sake of spending time doing what you enjoy.

Define the things you love about growing tomatoes (or anything else for that matter) and eliminate or automate everything else.

Apply It to Your Garden. First, let us remind you that *The 4-Hour Workweek* is the title of a book about business practices and, as such, shouldn't be taken literally. For most urban gardeners, four hours is a long time to spend in the garden, but the amount of time isn't the point.

Ferriss's concept was built on the idea that you could do the work of a forty-hour business week in just 10 percent of that time—four hours. With that in mind, see if you can reduce the time you invest in your garden down to just ten percent while actually improving your yield and your enjoyment.

Another integral part of the book is Pareto's law, which states that 80 percent of results are the outcome of 20 percent of the input. This works on both the positives and the negatives. Most of the time, 80 percent of our success comes from just 20 percent of the work we put in; 80 percent of our enjoyment lies in 20 percent of the activity we invest in; and 80 percent of the problems in our gardens are the result of 20 percent of the factors in our garden.

Our goal as urban gardeners should be to eliminate the 20 percent that causes problems, spend our time doing the 20 percent we enjoy, and automate everything else. In fact, this concept can and should be easily applied to nearly all areas of our lives, from gardening to parenting to office work to housework.

Now, get out there and enjoy your life!

Wrap It Up

In the next few chapters, we will introduce you to the basics of the Urban Garden Casual philosophy and how to implement it into your busy schedule. It can be done; it has been done before and you will succeed with your new urban garden. We are here to guide you through the entire process step by step so you can't lose! In each chapter, we have also chosen to spotlight some of our dear friends from all over the country—people who exemplify the very essence of urban gardening made casual. You will also find helpful tips, do-it yourself ideas, and other information throughout the book to keep you motivated!

What are you waiting for? Get out of your work clothes, turn on some music, grab a glass of wine, and let us show you how to garden, urban style!

2 Choose Your Urban Garden Casual Style

(Above) Photo by Kiley Goyette.

(Above) Photo by Frances Kuffel.

Before we get too deep into the nuts and bolts of the book, we need to first take a look at who we, the urban garden casual gardeners, are. Sure we could have just jumped headfirst into Gardening 101, but we think it is especially important for new gardeners to have an understanding of how who we are as people can have a tremendous effect on the plants we grow. Don't worry, we promise not to get too existential on you this early in the book.

In this chapter, we will evaluate your answers to these three questions:

1. What is the focus of my garden?
2. What is my gardening style?
3. What do I need to get my urban garden started?

Your Gardening Focus

Unlike our suburban and rural counterparts, an urban gardener does not have the luxury of a lack of focus. It is simple to see the need for this focused planning and direction when you look at the often severe space limitations and unique microclimates that are present in many urban garden settings. By having a clear understanding of your gardening purpose (your focus), you will be in a much better position to make a successful plan and execute that plan in a way that will maximize the space you have available and make it as beautiful as it can be.

When considering what your focus will be, you should start by asking yourself a few questions so you have a better understanding of what it is you need and/or want to accomplish with your pursuits.

23

Profiles in Casual: Ivette Soler

(Right) Photo by William Kaminski.

Location: Los Angeles, California
USDA Hardiness Zone: 10

Ivette Soler is a force to be reckoned with. A garden designer, consultant, and accomplished writer who studied acting at the California Institute of the Arts, she came about her love for gardening later in life than some, but she has more than made up for it over the past few years by devoting nearly every waking moment to what she calls the alchemy of gardening. One look at her work and you will appreciate the performance art she creates in gardens across the Los Angeles area.

"I started gardening because I hated what I was doing," Ivette says. It's interesting to note that at that point in her life, Ivette was acting—a tough career choice anywhere, but especially in Los Angeles. "When my husband, Jan, and I bought our first house, I was amazed at what gardening was. It really seemed like magic to me.

"I mean, you are really doing alchemy—bury a seed, add water and sun, and you get something incredible and beautiful and possibly edible! At that time in my life, I really needed that kind of wonder," Ivette explained. This sense of wonder led to her choose garden design and consulting as her new career.

"I've been kind of lucky in that I've had the opportunity to do big, over-the-top gardens in Los Angeles, but I have to say that my favorite spaces have always been the smaller ones that become a complete world. There is something extra special about walking into a jewel box of a garden that is balanced with a sense of fun, exuberance, but also with a sense of control—a unifying idea. Smaller spaces are easier to embrace in that way, so they hold a special place in my heart and my practice."

Soler's *go-big-or-go-home* attitude carries over into her own garden space as well—an area she considers to be her own outdoor laboratory.

"From the very beginning, I always looked to plants to figure out issues that most people would just use hardscapes for. For instance, I live one block away from a big high school, and kids would constantly cut across my corner lot. Everyone suggested that I put in a fence, but I wanted plants. I decided that mean, nasty, spiky agaves would be my fence. No more kids tearing through my front yard, and awesome beauty to boot."

How much time do you have to devote to your urban garden?

This is perhaps the most crucial of the focus questions. When dealing with container planting, it is absolutely imperative that the plants receive adequate (and frequent) water, or they won't survive. That doesn't mean you can't have an urban garden if you're busy; it just means that you need to look into the self-watering container options (covered in chapter 3) that will give you the freedom to go several days between watering.

Have you ever grown anything outdoors?

This isn't a pass-or-fail question, and you can still have a very successful garden if the answer is no. Heck, we have seen people who had never even owned a houseplant grow amazing rooftop gardens the first time they tried! In short, if the answer is no, then you need to start with veggies or flowering plants that are more forgiving to beginners (more on that in chapter 4). If the answer is yes, then you should be all set for moving forward by simply working on a plan and getting started.

Do you plan to eat what you grow or have a more visual garden?

While vegetable gardens are seeing the biggest surge in recent years, not everyone in larger cities eats at home, so vegetable plants wouldn't make much sense. Flowers and flowering plants can quickly and easily be cut and arranged into beautiful bouquets that can liven up a living space or become a meaningful gift for a friend or loved one.

Garden Like a Wine Taster

From WineCasual.com.

If you fancy yourself a wine taster like me (Reggie), chances are you might enjoy gardening like one as well. How, you ask? It's easier than you'd think.

Start by growing two or more types of each vegetable in your garden so you can compare and contrast tastes like a wine taster. In this way, you can build your palate to recognize and discern the subtleties in taste within a particular vegetable, fruit, or herb group.

You can conduct this experiment with every vegetable in your garden or choose two or three of your favorite vegetables with which to experiment.

At a wine tasting, you might try three wines made from the same Shiraz grape. When you taste the Shiraz grape in this format, you learn more about the grape's essence because you're comparing it with its cousins rather than with an entirely different grape family.

The same concept can be applied to vegetables in the urban garden. Rather than plant two of the same zucchini plant, use the same space to grow two different types—perhaps a globe-shaped zucchini or one that grows in the shape of a UFO saucer.

Don't be too concerned about buying two different packets of seeds for just a couple of plants. You can share seeds with neighbors, donate the extra to your local community garden, or save them to grow next year.

Imagine hosting a zucchini-tasting night when you serve one type of zucchini as an appetizer, another with the entrée, and still another type in fresh zucchini bread for dessert. And just for fun, why not serve two different Shirazes?

Your Gardening Style

No matter what your level of experience might be, there is no doubt that you will want your urban garden to match your style or at least to complement it. Are you the no-frills type who doesn't see much need for too much "stuff"? Maybe you are the artistic type who just can't resist adding your special flair to everything you do. It doesn't matter where you find yourself in the grand scheme of things; there is an urban gardening style that is perfectly suited for you.

With which of these style categories do you most closely identify?

The Brown Bagger

Brown Baggers takes their lunch to work every day and often eat the same foods out of familiarity. Their walls are usually white or off-white, and some people accuse them of being "bland" or "boring," though they don't see things that way. The fact is, they just don't feel the need to experiment with new or different things as long as the old things are working.

When it comes to gardening, the Brown Bagger generally sticks to the tried-and-true. They probably have a Big Boy tomato plant in a standard

round wire cage, some marigolds, and a few basic herbs in pots (basil, oregano, and chives if we had to venture a guess).

The Early Adopter

Early Adopters are always itching to try the next newest and best thing, even if it hasn't really been tested. They like to take risks because they believe the glory of success outweighs the gloom of failure. Early Adopters are never happy with the status quo, and they always go for more; if one is good, then five is amazing.

In the garden, the Early Adopter is just as cutting-edge, favoring the latest and greatest hybrid plants on the market, as well as the cool new garden gadgets like upside-down and vertical planters.

The Potlucker

Potluckers are the go-to people for new ideas. You can spot them because they seem to have subscriptions to every idea magazine imaginable. From Oprah to Martha, they have all the bases covered. They get their name because their dishes are always the talk of the potluck,

and they just got the recipe from a cooking show the day before. They always seem to have a new craft project in the works, or they are putting something into play that they have recently read about or seen on a TV show.

In the garden, the Potlucker is very visual—even more so than most. Their urban garden oasis will change with their whims as often as they find something eye-catching on a gardening show.

The Free Birder

Free Birders march to their own drum. No matter what area of their life you're talking about, they do it their way, no matter what, because—what the heck—life's supposed to be a learning experience, isn't it? The Free Birder was a recycler before recycling was cool (again).

In the garden, the Free Birder is not afraid of using an old paint bucket as an end table or of growing tomatoes on the front stoop, and they will laugh at the suggestion that they should buy something when they can repurpose an existing item. Free Birders are the most likely to have perfected the art of seed saving.

Sell Surplus at the Farmers Market

From UrbanGardenCasual.com.

You don't have to be a large-scale farmer to sell your produce at a farmers market. If you plan your garden carefully, you might just have enough of a surplus to sell at the market. Farmers markets aren't just for fresh produce, though. Canned preserves, jams and jellies, breads, homemade candies and desserts, and even dried herbs can be found at farmers markets around the country.

Urban gardeners can easily grow herbs to sell at the market. They can be grown quickly and easily, and the cost of most fresh herbs in the store has people seeking alternatives in open-air markets. Because herbs grow quickly and replenish themselves, you can conceivably grow several different herbs at once.

Contact the organizers for your local farmers market to learn about rules and costs for a booth rental.

Tomato Casual alum Amy Jeanroy, who is now the Herb Garden Guide for About.com, offers some great advice on getting ready for your farmers market selling adventure:

- Bring twice as much as you think you'll be able to sell. You will most likely sell out.
- Offer samples.
- Print recipe cards featuring the ingredients you sell.

Which Are You?

Having an understanding of your own gardening style will help you to better prepare for the all of the possibilities that arise in the urban garden environment and will help you to select plant varieties that will work best for you and bring you the most enjoyment. After all, if you don't enjoy it, why do it?

Making Your Urban Garden Casual

Now that you have figured out where you fit in the big picture, you can look further into your individual garden space at what you have to work with, what you can grow there, and what you need to make it all come together. This is where the real fun begins!

Evaluating Your Space

No matter what you have to work with, you can have a productive and great-looking urban garden, but you need to have realistic expectations based on the amount and type of space you have available. If all you have to work with is a shady stoop that doesn't get direct sunlight, then planting sun-hungry plants

(Above) Photo by Johanne Daoust.

like tomatoes or peppers is probably not going to lead to garden nirvana. Likewise, if you are gardening on your largely unprotected fire escape, you will probably need to take some precautions against the elements if your street acts like a wind tunnel.

Don't be disheartened by a perceived lack of space. If there is one lesson to be learned from life in the urban environment, it is that we sometimes have to be creative in finding and using every bit of space that is available, whether we initially realize it or not. Fire escapes, balconies, rooftops, and stoops are all good places for potential urban gardens, and even the traditional window box can be more flexible than you may have considered when you realize that it can be used indoors as well. Even the tightest of outdoor spaces may be able to house a vertical garden.

These factors are all quite important to consider in detail when evaluating your urban garden space:

Size. Let's face it, size does matter, but you can work with whatever you have available as long as you are realistic in your expectations. Measuring the actual dimensions of your space will give you a better handle on how much you can do. If you are—like most urban gardeners—dealing with container gardening, then you will need to know how many specific-sized containers you can fit into your space.

Take a look at the vertical space and how it might be used creatively to expand your overall usable garden space.

29

Conditions. What are the conditions like in your space? Do you get lots of sun, and if so, is it full sun or filtered? What about the wind? Tall buildings often create a wind tunnel microclimate that makes it difficult (but not impossible) for young seedlings to get a foothold, so be sure to consider these potential conditions before selecting plants and containers for your garden.

You should also realistically evaluate the amount of and proximity to foot traffic or general public access to your garden area because this may influence what you choose to grow and how you do so. An increase of foot traffic could also mean an increase in the potential for litter damage from discarded trash or cigarette butts. It might also mean a higher possibility of theft of the plants you are tending so faithfully.

When you select your plant types, sizes, and varieties, it's important to take into account the conditions you are working with.

Surrounding Décor. In most cases, you don't want your urban garden to stand out too much from its surroundings, so you need to make note of the area immediately surrounding your new garden. The goal is to integrate your garden as seamlessly as possible so your new urban garden space looks like it has been a part of the urban landscape for years. This is particularly important when your garden space is going to be visible to neighbors and the general public because you don't want your precious plants to become an eyesore for others.

See chapter 8 for a Garden Evaluation Worksheet that will help you plan your space and kick-start your creativity. This worksheet also is helpful to bring along to a garden center so you can ask for specific advice.

What to Grow?

After you have evaluated your space appropriately, you are ready to figure out what you will grow. You scrutinize the garden space first because you must fully understand

(Above) Photo by Kristine Paulus.

the area in which you will be planting. Then you can make informed choices about plants that will be easier to grow successfully in your specific space.

If you are gardening in containers, you need to first make sure that the plants you are growing are suited to container growing. Seeds and seedlings that have been specifically bred to do well in containers often are available. This is especially true of many fruit trees and vegetable varieties.

Here are a few plant suggestions that have been known to work well in containers:

Flowers and Bulbs. See the chart on page 32.

Vegetables. Most pepper plants will thrive in two to three gallon pots. As for tomatoes, we recommend varieties like Tiny Tim, Patio and Window Box Roma. Lettuces, cabbage, summer squash, radishes, and even potatoes can be easily grown in containers with a little extra care and attention. These days, deciding what to grow in your containers is more about personal preferences and time of year than anything else. Nearly anything that can be grown can be container grown.

Herbs. The majority of herbs you can find in the stores will thrive in containers, though you will need to choose varieties that will do well in your microclimate, so pay attention to each plant's needs as far as temperature and sunlight. Among our favorite herbs for containers are basil, chamomile, chives, oregano, rosemary, sweet mar-joram, and thyme, though most herbs are workable when given enough time and attention.

(Above) Photo by Reggie Solomon.

See the herb chart in chapter 5 for detailed information on a variety of herbs.

(Above) Photo by Reggie Solomon. (Above) Photo by Christine Polomsky for Horticulture Magazine/F+W Media.

FLOWER NAME	COLOR	PLANT SIZE	SUNLIGHT NEEDS	SKILL LEVEL
African daisy	variety	24"–36" (61cm–91cm)	full sun	easy
Asparagus fern	bright red berries	18"–24" (46cm–61cm)	partial to full sun	easy
Begonia	variety	6"–9" (15cm–23cm)	partial to full sun	easy
Bird-of-paradise	orange or white	depends on pot	full sun	moderate
Chrysanthemum	variety	8"–12" (20cm–30cm)	full sun	moderate
Columbine	variety	15"–20" (38cm–51cm)	partial sun	easy
Daffodil	yellow	12"–14" (30cm–36cm)	full sun	easy
Daylily	variety	12"–48" (30cm–122cm)	full sun	easy
Dutch hyacinth	violet	6"–12" (15cm–30cm)	partial to full sun	moderate
Lantana	variety	36"–48" (91cm–122cm)	full sun	easy
Lamb's ear	violet	6"–12" (15cm–30cm)	partial to full sun	easy
Marigold	red, orange, gold	6"–12" (15cm–30cm)	full sun	easy
Zinnia	variety	36"–48" (91cm–122cm)	full sun	easy

Plants That Attract Nature

From UrbanGardenCasual.com.

Hummingbirds

One of the most beloved birds in the world is the tiny, vibrant hummingbird. They are also one of the most commonly sought after creatures for backyard bird-watchers around the country. Thousands of people have invested in hummingbird feeders in the hopes of capturing a glimpse from time to time. Why not ditch those old, boring, and messy feeders in favor of what these aviary beauties really crave? These plants are excellent natural hummingbird magnets:

Sunset Hyssop. All of the hyssops that have pink or orange flowers attract hummingbirds, but our favorite is Sunset hyssop. These flowers are a brilliant mixture of orange, purple and pink. This plant has a splendid scent often described as licorice or root beer. Once the hyssop is established, it is quite drought resistant as well.

Hummingbird Trumpet. These stunning trumpet-shaped flowers come in shades of red or orange. They also have the advantage of being drought resistant once established.

Azaleas. These standbys of any good Southern garden space are a favorite for a reason—they attract hummingbirds with their vibrant blooms, and they are quite easy to grow.

Gladiolus. These pretty flowers grow from *corms* (similar to bulbs) and are available in a dazzling array of colors. An added bonus is that each gladiolus will produce additional corms each year, so at the end of the season you can dig them up, divide them, and plant even more gladiolus the next year.

33

(Left) Photo by Al Parrish for Horticulture Magazine/F+W Media.

(Left) Photo by Reggie Solomon.

Our readers at UrbanGardenCasual.com chimed in with some of their favorites as well:

- Honeysuckle
- Petunia
- Calibrachoa
- Salvia (both red and purple)
- Cleome
- Autumn sage
- Lantana
- Scarlet Runner pole beans

Butterflies

Butterflies are beautiful, serene, and delicate. They add so much to the outdoor environment, and yet they make no noise, leave no waste, and require so little in return for the joy they provide. Here are a few basic tips to help bring butterflies into your yard or garden space:

Whenever possible, put plants in full sun. When choosing your plants, try to pick the ones that grow in full sun because this is the kind of lighting most favorable for butterfly feeding. Talk to a professional at your local garden center or nursery for the full-sun plants that will grow best in your area.

Avoid the use of pesticides and insecticides. When you think of pesticides, you think of all the undesirable insects that munch away on your plants. However, these pesticides are not picky and will work on any insect— even butterflies. Use alternative ways to deal with specific insect problems.

Encourage butterfly caterpillars. Caterpillars are the young form of butterflies. They can be very picky about which plants they will eat. Talk to your garden professional to find out what plants in your area are best for caterpillars.

(Above) Photo by Christine Polomsky for Horticulture Magazine/F+W Media.

(Above) Photo by Reggie Solomon

Choose plants that attract butterflies. By far, the easiest way to bring butterflies to your garden is to plant species that they like to eat nectar from. Attracting the beautiful creatures to your garden all summer long is easy if you create a butterfly garden using any of these butterfly favorites:

- Butterfly bush / *Buddleia davidii*
- Butterfly milkweed / *Asclepias tuberose*
- Hibiscus / *Hibiscus huegelii*
- Hollyhock / *Althaea rosea*
- Nasturtium / *Tropaeolum majus*
- Queen Anne's lace / *Daucus carota*
- Sage / *Salvia species*
- Yarrow / *Achillea species*

If you are container gardening, you don't have to exclude yourself from the beauty of a butterfly garden. Simply grow a selection of annuals and perennials that thrive in container environments and you will have fluttering beauties in no time. Many plants are perfect for smaller gardens and can be easily grown in pots.

Container-ready annuals include: marigolds, nasturtiums, nicotiana, New England asters, and butterfly milkweed.

Container-ready perennials include: thyme, sage, rosemary, lavender, lemon balm, chives, black-eyed Susans, marsh hibiscus, lobelia, and Shasta daisies.

Butterflies need a source of water. Butterflies don't drink directly from pools of water, but stand on mud or damp sand and drink from the earth. They also get trace minerals by doing this.

A cheap and easy way to provide water for your butterflies is to create a butterfly lick. Just fill a terra cotta dish with sand and organic black earth soil mixed together and keep it very damp all summer long. If you already have a

water feature, such as a pond or bubble fountain, add a few rocks wedged into the dirt surrounding it to give butterflies a good place to stand and sip water.

As the plant lists show, attracting butterflies can be as easy as adding a few herbs and flowers in pots to your existing garden. Creating a small garden filled with plants butterflies love will allow you to watch these elegant creatures all summer long.

The Casual Tools

Urban gardeners are an interesting and diverse lot. There are those who can grow a veritable cornucopia that will feed their family all year for just a few dollars (the Free Birder) and then there are the ones who spend a fortune to grow just a few plants because they are following trends or the latest and most expensive accoutrements (the Potlucker or Early Adopter). The purpose of this section is to give you a short rundown on the tools we have found to be indispensable. (As much as we would like to give you the dirt on a few real stinkers we have tried over the years, we really don't want to risk a lawsuit at this point in our careers.)

The Basics. A good trowel and a pair of gardening gloves should be at the top of your must-have list. You'll also be well served by a wide-brimmed hat for the beautiful, bright sunny days. A small foam cushion will prove invaluable, as you will no doubt want to save your knees from the long-term kneeling you'll be doing.

In addition, be sure to check out:

Fiskars Garden Bucket Caddy. An ingenious design, this canvas caddy fits over a five-gallon bucket and has various pockets and holsters for holding not only your necessary

gardening tools, but also a drink, your keys, even your cell phone! The design leaves the center of the bucket empty and open, perfect for larger tools or a place to hold your bounty.

Hori Hori Garden Knife. We wouldn't even think about going into our gardening spaces without a Hori Hori. Shaped like a long shovel, this knife has a serrated edge that is great for getting rid of pesky weeds. It is also handy for planting bulbs and removing stubborn roots. We dare you to find another single tool that will give you as many uses in the garden.

Oxo Good Grips Garden Scissors. If we had to tend and harvest our herbs without these dreamy scissors, we might think twice about planting so many! The wide grips make them extra-comfortable, and the serrated edge makes simple work of cutting through even the toughest stems like rosemary and oregano.

**Oxo Good Grips
Garden Scissors**

The best part? They work equally well whether you are left- or right-handed.

Fiskars Garden Bucket Caddy

These tools are by no means the only options available, nor are they the only ones you will need. For that reason, specific tools are suggested throughout this book as they are called for. By the same token, if you find a brand or type of tool that you're more comfortable with, go with what works for you. Gardening is an individual pursuit, and it should be as enjoyable and familiar as possible. Don't waste time using tools that don't suit your needs.

Wrap It Up

In this chapter, we looked not only at what we want to grow, but also at how the area we garden in may be affected by such things as climate and foot traffic. We took a look at ourselves and dug deep to find out what our gardening personality is and how it can impact our choices as urban gardeners.

(Above) Photo by Andrew Miller.

3 Casual Container Gardening

Containers are at the center of most urban gardens. They make it possible to grow a tremendous variety of plants in areas that typically aren't very plant-friendly. They also allow you to grow plants in areas that either don't naturally have the right type of soil or don't have soil at all. The order of the day is flexibility, and when it comes to urban container gardening, that is exactly what you get.

The charts and lists in chapters 2 and 5 show just a few of the many possible plants you can grow in containers, but don't let them be anything more than a guide! Talk to experts in your area to find out what container plants will work best where you live. Many plants are bred for specific conditions, such as temperature and other climate variations, so there are bound to be a few that will work better for you than they do for us.

Each year brings an onslaught of brand-new plant varieties that are specifically created to thrive in containers. This is especially beneficial to those would-be urban gardeners who want to grow veggies but had been wary of trying before. The Patio tomato, for example, is a mighty little powerhouse that is tailor-made to be

pot-bound and will reward you with tons of beautiful fruit throughout the season.

We all know that containers make it possible to green up your indoor living space, but why stop there when you can use container gardening techniques to grow virtually anything outdoors as well? From plain-Jane terra cotta to high-end, prefab, self-watering containers and everything in between, there is sure to be a container combination that will work perfectly in your situation and with the space you have available.

Choosing Your Container

Planters come in a mind-numbing array of sizes, styles, colors, finishes, and materials, but not all containers are created equal. Just because a container exists doesn't necessarily mean it is right for your needs. You need to take a few factors into consideration when choosing your container.

Climate and weather can have a tremendous impact on the containers you choose, especially if it can be exceptionally cold or wet where the containers will be placed. Some wooden and metal containers, for example, may not fare quite so well if they are repeatedly exposed to heavy rains and subfreezing temperatures. Untreated wood can rot more quickly than you might have imagined, and some metal containers will rust and fall apart over time, exposing dangerous sharp edges and potentially spelling disaster for your precious urban garden.

The most common problem people have with using containers is that they don't know how to choose the right ones for their purposes. For example, soil in containers tends to dry out more quickly than ground soil, a point that has been at the root of the problems many urban gardeners have when using containers. In recent years, at least two possible options have presented themselves, and both are affordable and attractive.

Self-watering containers are an excellent solution for the forward-thinking types who are starting their urban gardening pursuits from scratch. These containers are available in a variety of shapes, sizes, and colors that are sure to complement any garden style. There are some popular brands available on the market, and a quick Internet search will make it easy to find them if you're looking to purchase one. Alternatively, you might even consider making your own self-watering garden containers, and you will save quite a bit of money in the process.

Though the design specifics vary, most self-watering containers work under the same basic principle. A false bottom is filled with water that is in turn wicked into the soil above it as needed to keep the plants well watered and thriving. A watering tube makes it possible to easily refill the water reservoir as necessary. If well constructed and well maintained, a self-watering garden container can be used and reused for years to come, making the investment well worth it, whether you purchase or make one yourself. For instructions on how to make your own self-watering

tip Although containers serve a practical purpose, that doesn't mean they have to necessarily look practical. In fact, some of our favorite containers don't look like plant containers at all. You can use nearly anything imaginable, after taking a few precautionary steps. To get the look you want, simply place sturdy, less-expensive pots inside your decorative, more-expensive-looking containers.

(Above) Photo by Kristine Paulus.

Build Your Own Self-Watering Container

From UrbanGardenCasual.com.

You can make your own inexpensive, self-watering container with just a little work.

You'll need:

- Two five-gallon buckets (Don't use ones that have held chemicals. Make sure the containers can fit inside each other.)
- Drill
- Wick (Cotton is a good choice. You can buy a piece of cotton cord or rope or even use an old T-shirt.)
- Hacksaw
- PVC pipe, 3"–4" (8cm–10cm) longer than the height of your inner bucket
- Utility knife
- Potting mix (the kind that retains moisture is ideal)

How to build the container:

1. Place the buckets inside each other to see how much room you have for water in the bottom. Mark where the inside bucket ends on the side of the outside bucket. You can use short lengths of extra PVC pipe (2"–3" [5cm–8cm]) or rocks to prop up the inner bucket if you want more room for water.
2. Cut a length of PVC pipe with the hacksaw that is an inch or two (3cm–5cm) longer than the height of the stacked buckets. Cut one end at a 45-degree angle so water will be able to reach the reservoir easier. Separate the buckets.
3. Drill a hole just below your mark on the outside bucket. This will serve as an overflow drain so you know when the reservoir is full.

4. Drill several small holes in the bottom of the inner bucket so oxygen can reach the roots. Keep the holes small

enough that the soil will stay in the bucket. Now create two larger holes in the bottom of the inner bucket. The first needs to be large enough to snugly accommodate a piece of PVC pipe. The second larger hole should be near the middle of the inner bucket. It should be large enough that the wick will barely fit through it.
5. Thread the wick through the hole in the bottom. Make sure it is long enough to reach both the bottom of the water reservoir and into the soil.
6. Place the buckets together. Fit the PVC pipe into the hole you created. This will allow you to fill the water reservoir.
7. Carefully fill the inner bucket with potting mix and add your plant. Make sure to bring the wick up into the soil.
8 Use the PVC tube to add water until it starts coming out of the overflow hole. Also, water the plant on top to get the moisture system started.

Presto! You now have a self-watering container. How often you need to fill it depends on how hot the weather is and what plants you are growing (tomatoes can be very thirsty indeed!), but overall it will make life much easier.

(Above) Photo by Carol Bunch.

container, visit UrbanGardenCasual.com and search for "self-watering container" or see the sidebar on page 44.

Already have a container that you love? No worries; you can help your plants water themselves whether you are going away for a few days or are just too forgetful to remember to water periodically. You have likely seen the brand-name product Aqua Globes advertised on television in the last few years. We laughed at them the first time we saw them, thinking the idea ridiculous. Then Michael was given a pair as a gift and gave them a try, and now he recommends them to anyone who has the need. They

work exactly as advertised, and they even look like jewelry in your planters.

Also important when selecting a container is to take into consideration the mature size of the plant or plants you want to put into it. When you buy those cute vegetable plants at the store, they are far from mature. The majority of vegetables will need to establish a deep root system, and some, like cucumbers, squash and zucchini, need either plenty of room to spread out or something vertical to climb on. Detailed information on specific climbing plants is covered in chapter 5.

Getting to Know Hypertufa

It may sound like something you'd go to a specialist to have removed, but in reality, hypertufa is a hyper-cool manmade or *anthropic* rock substance that is so easy to mix and mold you can do it yourself. Why would you want to? Simple! Make your own hypertufa, and you can make your own planters!

We know it sounds like it could get pretty complicated, but hypertufa is a basic mixture that includes just three things: three parts Portland cement, four parts peat moss, and five parts perlite. By adding water to those ingredients and pouring it into a mold, you can make containers in a huge variety of sizes and styles, from refined to natural and everything in between.

For more information on hypertufa and to find instructions on how to make your own, visit UrbanGardenCasual.com and search for "hypertufa."

Types of Containers

Terra Cotta

Terra cotta may be the most traditional and the most common type of pots, but they are not without their own set of problems. They are quite porous, so they absorb a lot of water and can pull water from the soil inside of them. They also are known to dry out quickly, and they can crack and sometimes even shatter when they absorb moisture and subsequently freeze. Still, they have a style all their own and have been used successfully in urban container gardens all over the country for more years than we'll admit to being alive.

To select the best terra cotta containers, purchase only those that offer a guarantee that they are frost proof (not just frost resistant). To check the pot's quality, thump the side of the pot with your fingernail. A slight ringing is a good sign that the pot is in good condition, while a flat thud means the pot has cracks, even if you cannot see them.

Finally, it is a good idea to soak terra cotta pots in water prior to planting in them to ensure that the container does not pull necessary moisture away from

(Above) Photo by Catherine Macdonald.

(Above) Photo courtesy of Jenny White, Activity Club.

your plants. Alternatively you might consider lining the inside of the pot with plastic, but be sure to leave the drainage holes exposed.

Metal

Metal containers have become increasingly sought after in the past few years for their modern, minimalist appearance. They are an excellent option for casual urban gardeners who are looking for clean lines and a sleek look to complement their style.

green tip Don't throw away the small, plastic pots your plants come in from the garden center or nursery. Clean them thoroughly, and they are ready to be reused, especially when you begin starting your own seeds and need to "pot up" from your seed starting trays.

It is important to note that metal is a good conductor of both heat and cold. As such, you must take precautions to ensure that the plant roots aren't cooked in hot weather or frozen in the cold. Oddly enough, we have had luck using bubble wrap as an insulator between the metal container and the plastic insert that we use to contain the plant material.

Ceramics

Ceramics are well-known for being brightly colored and patterned with an assortment of glazes and finishing techniques. They offer a more finished and refined look for those who seek such things, and by nature, the glaze will often keep moisture from getting through the surface to the clay, making them frost proof by default.

Still, it is strongly recommended that you check ceramic pots thoroughly, looking for any blisters, scratches or crazing of the glaze because that will mean a compromise of the moisture barrier that could result in cracks or shattering.

(Left) Photo by Reggie Solomon.

Plastic

Plastic containers are not only easy to find, lightweight, and flexible, but they are usually quite inexpensive when compared to their wooden, stone, or metal counterparts. Most plastic pots can be painted easily with simple acrylic paints as a way to add life and your signature style to your urban garden. Although the light-weight feature of plastic is beneficial when you are faced with moving containers, it could end up being a disadvantage if your garden space is in a windy location, so take steps to ensure that your lightweight planters are secure and won't tip or spill.

The best plastic containers for urban gardeners will be labeled as "UV-stabilized." This is definitely worth looking for because pots without this designation often become brittle and quickly lose all strength when exposed to sunlight and the elements.

Wood

It's easy to have an affinity for containers made of wood, such as hardwood barrels like those used in the making of whiskey or wine. These are an excellent choice for outdoor planting because they are naturally resistant to rotting, and they offer plenty of room for strong root development on your more-vigorous growers like tomatoes, cucumbers, and squash.

If your wooden container is made of a soft wood, you should waterproof the inside with a preservative that is nontoxic and harmless to your plants. Talk to a professional at your local garden center to get specific product recommendations that are best for your needs. Don't forget to seal the outside as well, using whatever you like, from porous paint to colored stain.

Recycled Containers

Recycled containers are one of the most creative ideas we have come across in recent years. Find truly unique items to repurpose as containers for your urban garden. Over the years we have seen everything from old tires and wagons to toilets (yes, really) and old bicycles with the baskets filled with beautiful blooms. If you put your creativity to work, the possibilities are truly endless, and you can end up with some one-of-a-kind creations that will be the envy of the neighborhood.

Need a few ideas to get you started? Look around for old metal mop buckets, wicker baskets, even cat litter pails, enamelware containers, washtubs, and wine casks. Let your creativity run wild and see what you can create from the items around you.

Stone

For hundreds of years, stone containers have been used all over the world as planters, and that trend has never really shown signs of letting up. Now there are replicas of antique-era, carved-stone garden containers that are both easier to work with and less expensive. Even manmade

(Right) Photo by www.sustainableecho.com.

(Right) Photo by Ric Deliantoni.

(Left) Photo by Justin Martin.

stone, called *anthropic* rock (see the sidebar on page 46), can be used to create amazing planters. Manmade stone containers also often have the benefit of being lighter weight than their natural counterparts.

Raised Beds

Raised beds are another possibility, if you have the space available to make them work. In short, a raised bed is a bed that is most often constructed atop existing earth, though it is sometimes constructed on concrete slabs or even asphalt or another hard surface. In essence, the raised bed is a large container. Because of that, the same basic rules that apply to containers will apply to raised beds, just on a slightly larger scale. For example, you might have a long, narrow alleyway-type space to work with, and a grouping of smaller containers—while attractive—might not make the best and most productive use of the space. A raised bed might be just what the garden doctor ordered.

We've seen successful raised beds on rooftops and in narrow passageways between townhome patios, so we are absolutely sure they can work for you. Always remember that proper drainage is crucial, and you'll be off and running in no time.

If cost is a concern for you, check sites like Craigslist and your local Freecycle mailing list where you often can find people who are giving away old wood from torn-down fences and buildings. Even in less-than-perfect condition, free wood is a good deal. When Joe Lamp'l started his $25 Victory Garden Challenge in 2009, he got his wood through a Freecycle connection. (Read more about Craigslist and Freecycle in chapter 8.)

Plant Selection

It doesn't take a rocket scientist to understand that some plants are just not well suited to containers. Plants that need plenty of room to stretch and expand are almost always going to give you a fit if you put them in a potted prison. No worries, my plant-seeking friends; there is no shortage of plants that are prime for your urban garden containers. Take a look at the charts in chapters 2 and 5 for a quick reference on the details of various veggies, flowers and herbs.

For best results, look to plants that don't take too long to mature. They should have a solid growing season and

USDA Hardiness Zone Map

The United States Department of Agriculture (or USDA as it is more commonly known) created the Hardiness Zone Map to describe different geographically defined areas that have similar climate characteristics. There are eleven identified zones on the map. The zones stretch across several states with changes in climate marking where one zone ends and another begins. Seed and plant companies often label their plants with the zone numbers in which the plants will thrive best. That makes selecting your plants as easy as looking up your zone number and checking the plant labels. A plant that is identified as growing well in Zone 7 will grow well in any area that is designated by the map as Zone 7.

ZONE	AVG ANNUAL MIN TEMP	EXAMPLE CITIES
1	Below -50°F (-45.6°C)	Fairbanks, Alaska
2	-50 to -40°F (-45.5 to -40°C)	Prudhoe Bay, Alaska; Unalakleet, Alaska
3	-40 to -30°F (-39.9 to 34.5°C)	International Falls, Minnesota; Sidney, Montana
4	-30 to -20°F (-34.4 to -28.9°C)	Minneapolis; Omaha, Nebraska
5	-20 to -10°F (-23.4 to -26.1°C)	Chicago; Columbus, Ohio
6	-10 to -5°F (-23.3 to -17.8°C)	Philadelphia; St. Louis; Nashville
7	0 to 10°F (-17.7 to -12.3°C)	New York City; Baltimore; Atlanta
8	10 to 20°F (-12.2 to -6.7°C)	Dallas; Seattle; Phoenix, Arizona
9	20 to 30°F (-6.6 to -1.2°C)	Houston; Orlando, Florida
10	30 to 40°F (-1.1 to 4.4°C)	Los Angeles; Miami
11	above 40°F (above 4.5°C)	Honolulu, Hawaii

be able to withstand occasional drought conditions (hey, you're not perfect, and you don't want your plant babies to die because you forget them once). It helps to know your USDA Hardiness Zone before you begin selecting plants. If you don't know your zone designation, you can find resources in the chapter 8 that will get you headed in the right direction in no time.

You would think the garden department in the home improvement big-box stores would only carry plants that are appropriate and hardy in your area, but this is not always the case. Always check the plant label and don't be afraid to ask questions if you are unsure about a particular plant. If you can't get the answers you need at the store, it is a good time to find another source for your plants and information. This is precisely why we always recommend that you find a local nursery and develop a rapport with the staff.

Planting in Containers

Regardless of the type of container you choose, the general rules of engagement will remain the same for nearly any container planting application. First, your chosen vessel must allow for adequate drainage, or you risk all sorts of problems ranging from root rot to mold, none of which are fun to deal with. If you have found a container that does not already have drainage holes, you can usually rectify the problem. You can carefully drill holes in the bottoms of plastic containers. Metal containers may fare well with a hammer and nail. Before you do anything else, make absolutely sure that your container has good drainage holes. Without them, you are setting yourself up to fail.

Is Wheatgrass the New Catnip?

From UrbanGardenCasual.com.

Wheatgrass is considered a superfood because it is loaded with vitamins, minerals, enzymes and chlorophyll. It boosts the immune system and helps give some serious health power to your morning smoothie, too. Perhaps the most important benefit to the amazing wheatgrass, though, is that cats love the stuff.

Growing your own wheatgrass is much cheaper than the cutesy grow-your-own cat grass packets sold in pet stores or the trays of fresh wheatgrass in the produce department of fancy grocery stores. For a dollar or two a pound, you can find whole wheat berries at nearly any natural health-food store in the country. Depending on where you are, the berries that are available may be red or white, and either will work so long as they are whole and raw. Cracked wheat berries taste good, but they will not germinate.

If you're growing wheatgrass for kitty purposes, fill a 6" (15cm) diameter pot with all-purpose potting mix, plus a little compost thrown in if you have it. If you're growing wheatgrass for yourself, use a 12" × 12" (30cm × 30cm) greenhouse tray instead so you'll have enough wheatgrass to juice for several smoothies.

Measure out enough wheat berries to densely cover your pot or tray (two tablespoons is good for a 6" [15cm] pot) and soak them overnight in an open jar of water. The next morning, drain the seeds and sow them in your pot or tray, just barely covering them with potting mix. Stick the pot in a warm, sunny window and water once a day or as needed to keep the soil evenly moist.

The wheatgrass is ready to harvest when it is at least 6" (15cm) tall, about ten days after planting. You can snip

(Left) Photo by Ric Deliantoni.

off leaves and add them to your cat's food, or you can just let your cat graze directly from the pot. Limit kitty's access to the wheatgrass at first because some cats get an upset tummy from eating too many greens.

Getting Your Container Ready

After you have checked your container for proper drainage and made any necessary adjustments, you will need to ensure that the drainage hole is guarded—a process called "crocking"—to prevent the potting soil from going AWOL. This is really a simple matter of placing a small stone or piece of a broken pot or dish over the drainage hole prior to filling the container with potting mix. If your container is large, you might consider taking up some of the unnecessary space at the bottom with broken pieces of Styrofoam or even old disposable coffee cups before filling it with potting soil mixture. This will save you money on soil and has the added benefit of making the finished container a lot lighter.

The Right Potting Mix

Next, the soil used in containers must be light and airy. Soil in this condition not only allows for proper drainage, but also allows for the proper oxygen flow to the roots. There are plenty of good-quality potting soil mixes on the market, and making a decision might seem like a difficult task, but don't let yourself get overwhelmed. The pros at any reputable garden center will be able to steer you in the right direction so you can choose the perfect potting mix for your needs.

If the potting mix you choose is dry, you should wet it thoroughly before you plant in it. It should be damp and just shy of a muddy consistency. This will make the transition from seedling pot to your new container much less stressful on the plant and much more rewarding for you. It will also make it easier to ensure a thorough soaking for all of those young, tender roots.

Profiles in Casual: Mike Lieberman

(Right) Photo by Mike Lieberman.

Location: New York City
USDA Hardiness Zone: 7

Mike Lieberman is an ultra-cool, straight talkin' Brooklynite who happens to grow some of his own food. From his fire escape in the village to his grandma's backyard in Brooklyn, Mike is always working to make the most of the space and resources he has available. Whether creating his own self-watering containers or testing soil pH by giving it a taste test, Mike is as fearless in the garden as he is in daily life. Even we haven't been adventurous enough to pee on our tomato plants.

Why did you first become an urban gardener?

I started urban gardening because I was told that I couldn't do it because I live in New York City, and I wanted to prove the naysayers wrong. Now I do it because it's good for the environment, helps me to better connect with my food and cuts into my grocery bills.

What are your favorite plants to grow?

I like greens and lettuces because they grow pretty quickly and continue to grow. I eat a lot of salads, so it's the quick gratification of harvesting my own meals.

What's your favorite container?

Five-gallon buckets are the base of most of my containers. Like I said, I do this for environmental reasons as well, so I build my containers out of recycled materials.

(Above) Photo by Mike Lieberman.

(Left) Photo by Tina Negus.

Mulching and Containers

You are probably thinking, "Mulch? Why do I need mulch in a flower pot?" The simple fact is that container-bound plants need mulch even more so than their ground-planted cousins. Containers are notorious for drying out faster than the ground, so a good mulch is crucial to the success of your urban container garden.

What should you use as mulch? Well, that's where the fun begins because container mulch can be a lot more flexible than ground-covering mulch. Sure, you could be traditional and use bark, cedar chips, or pine straw, if you are so inclined, but you could just as easily use small stones, pebbles, or even marbles to add some visual interest to your potted creations. What you use as mulch is less important than using *something*.

Over the years we have used everything from dried flowers and leaves to shells, Spanish moss, and even wine corks. Whatever your mulching medium, make sure that it does its job by helping to retain moisture and keeping the potting soil in the container where it belongs.

Companion Planting

One of the earliest gardening lessons we learned was the importance of companion planting in the garden. In short, the concept refers to the symbiotic nature that some plant combinations can have when grown together. In some cases, this symbiosis is beneficial for protection against insects or climate, while at other times it is strictly for visual appeal. The power of companion planting should not be ignored when planning your container garden.

There's an old concept that's been around seemingly forever that refers specifically to planting a container:

(Above) Photo by Al Parrish for Horticulture Magazine/F+W Media.

Thrill, fill, and spill. This concept, when carefully applied by using plants that work well together, makes it easy to create stunning containers that will have everyone asking who is your designer.

Thrill. The visual height and eye-catching part of a container planting. Some examples of thrillers might be begonias or snapdragons.

Fill. The plant or plants that fill out the middle section of the planter. Two great fillers are impatiens and lavender.

Spill. A plant that hangs or spills over the side of the container. Ivy or sweet potato vines are great spillers.

For more on this topic, there is an entire section in chapter 5 devoted to companion planting for optimum tomato production.

Wrap It Up

In this chapter, we have looked at containers and the tremendous variety and flexibility that they offer. We explored the different options for container materials, as well as how to prepare a container for planting in the urban garden environment. We introduced the USDA Hardiness Zone Map and explained why it is important. You should have a good idea of the type of containers you will use and how to properly prepare your containers, and you should know the USDA Hardiness Zone in which you live.

tip Unsure about the needs of specific plants? Check with a local garden expert or ask us at UrbanGardenCasual.com.

4 Getting Started

Now that we have some of the formalities out of the way, we are going to take a look at what you need to do to get started working in your urban garden environment and, equally as important, *when* you need to do it. All too often, would-be gardeners try to take on too much too quickly, and then they find themselves overwhelmed by a project that didn't need to be as complicated as it ended up being. By keeping just a few basic concepts in mind, you will find yourself closer than ever to having an urban garden that is the envy of all who see it.

Site Preparation

Container gardeners can skip this section because it applies particularly to those who are preparing for an in-ground or raised bed urban garden site, or for those working within the confines of a community garden plot.

Preparing your new garden site is a crucial step in the process and one that you cannot afford to skip or carry out in a haphazard way. The area must be ready to take on the burden of new plantings, and the soil must have the necessary amendments in the form of compost, fertilizer, and other potentially necessary additives to give your new garden the head start it will need to ensure success throughout the growing season. For starters, let's take a look at the type of soil you will be working with and the condition it is currently in.

What's Your Soil Type?

In order to prepare existing soil for successful urban gardening, you must first ascertain what type of soil you have. This will enable you to add the right amendments that are needed to grow strong and healthy plants. Scientifically speaking, there are several aspects of the soil that are important including color, compaction, content (both moisture and organic), pH, profile, structure, temperature, and texture. For our purposes, we don't need to get all that scientific, so we will take a quick look at only those aspects that are important to us at this point.

There are three general types of soil that you might encounter, and each carries its own benefits and potential challenges. Your existing soil will ideally be a good mix of

the three—sand, silt, and clay—but even if it isn't perfect (most aren't), you can take measures to make it right.

Soil texture refers to the size of the individual particles. The three basic kinds (sand, silt, and clay) are all found in your soil in different degrees.

Sand has the largest particles of the three. It's great for plants that don't like to have wet roots because it drains very well. That also means, though, that water-loving plants may have problems because the water leaves quickly, taking nutrients with it.

Silt is the middle kind of texture. It's a good standard for most plants.

Clay has the smallest particles. They are very close together, and clay holds water for a while after being irrigated, which causes problems for some plants. It does hold nutrients better, though. One way to improve clay soil is to add organic material like compost.

A mixture of all three kinds is called loam, and loam is the stuff of gardeners' dreams. It combines the positive aspects of all three soil types.

The easiest way to get an approximate idea of what kind of soil texture is present in your garden is to simply grab a moist handful and squeeze!

- If it doesn't really stick together at all, you have sand.
- If it forms a loose ball that you can still break apart, you have silt.
- If it forms a firm ball, you have clay.

Soil Color. You can quickly tell quite a bit about your soil based on how dark or light the color of it is. Fertile soil

that is rich in organic matter and nitrogen will be darker in color, while lighter-colored soil will generally be less organic, carry less oxygen, and require more aeration. Lighter-colored soils are also more prone to erosion.

Here is a quick explanation of the terms in the chart at right for those who may not be familiar with them:

- **Aeration** refers to the airiness of the soil, or how much air can flow through the particles in the soil and reach the roots.
- **Humus** is not to be confused with the delicious edible dip of a similar name. In this case, we are referring to a dark, rich, earthy soil layer that is comprised of well-decayed organic matter. In easier-to-understand terms, humus is created during the composting process.

- **Nitrogen** is a naturally occurring chemical element that is a major component in chlorophyll. It is largely responsible for the deep green color of many plants and is a key ingredient in healthy plant

SOIL COLOR			
Soil Condition	**Very Dark**	**Fairly Dark**	**Light**
Aeration	Good	Moderate	Low
Degree of Fertility	Good	Moderate	Low
Erosion Potential	Low	Moderate	Good
Humus Content	Good	Moderate	Low
Nitrogen Content	Good	Moderate	Low

The Most Popular Urban Garden in America

When first lady Michelle Obama announced her intention to start a kitchen garden on the White House lawn, some people called it a groundbreaking move. While it was inspired to be sure, Mrs. Obama was actually taking a page from a much older playbook. Before her, Eleanor Roosevelt was the most recent resident of 1600 Pennsylvania Avenue to plant a garden. Mrs. Roosevelt planted hers during the World War II Victory Garden movement, but even she wasn't the first. In fact, the tradition of gardening at the White House has its true roots as early as 1800 when President John Adams is said to have had a garden at the country's most well-known address.

growth. Nitrogen is created naturally during the breakdown of organic elements in the soil, but it can also be added in fertilizers and other soil additives.

To gauge your soil color, dig down about 3"–4" (8cm–10cm) and take a look at the soil you find there. Look at the color before the sun has a chance to dry it out, or you might not be accurate in your assessment.

Soil Compaction. The more compact your soil is, the less air can circulate through it. Overly compacted soil is usually high in clay content and lacks the proper circulation of air and water. New root systems have a difficult time establishing themselves in compact soil. As a result, plants that are grown in this soil condition will likely experience stunted growth and, in the case of vegetable and fruit plants, a lower than normal rate of production.

You can (if you feel it is necessary) check the level of compaction in your ground soil in just a few minutes using little more than an old metal coffee can and a timer. Use a can opener to cut the bottom out of the can so you have a completely open cylinder. Use a ruler and a black permanent marker to mark the inside of the can in 1" (3cm) increments from the top to the bottom. Next, push the can into the soil until it is 3" (8cm) deep (you can use a small board and a mallet or hammer if needed).

When your tester can is in place, fill it with water to the very top and then sit back and watch. Check the water level every 60 seconds for 10 minutes, keeping a record of your findings. At the end of 10 minutes, divide the total number of inches (or centimeters) that have drained away by 10. This information can be quite helpful when determining the proper amount of water needed in a specific area.

Profiles in Casual: Shala and James Cross

Location: Texas
USDA Hardiness Zone: 8

In yet another testament to the far-reaching fingers of social media, Michael first met Shala and James Cross on Twitter in 2009 through an amazing network of friends and fellow gardeners. This odd couple couldn't be more different, but they share a common bond that helps bring them closer to each other, one growing season at a time.

Growing up, Shala and James were both heavily influenced by gardening. Their grandparents all were avid gardeners (Shala's maternal grandfather was a farmer), and so it would just make sense that growing a garden would come naturally for this young Texas couple. It wasn't always easy for them, though.

"When we first got married, we lived in apartments, and the movement of balcony gardening really hadn't blossomed as it has now—so we had very little to show for our love of gardening. Since buying our first home—and now our second—our love for gardening has taken off," James said. "The time we spend together in the garden is a time that other married couples just simply do not have."

That time is quite productive, with the couple taking advantage of the climate in Texas to grow lots of hot-weather-friendly plants, such as peppers and tomatoes.

"We have found that other couples get excited when we start talking about everything we grow, about our local farmers market or whatever else we have going on in regards to gardening/urban farming. Family and friends read our website and try things they never have before, or are getting into it because of an article we linked to that pointed out something they haven't thought about."

James is also a huge fan of grilling, barbecuing, and "just about anything that involves bacon." The pair's passion for gardening has even led James to design and build several unique items for their planting pursuits. Not one to keep such things to himself, he uses the couple's site, DoubleDanger.com, to share photos, shopping lists, and even step-by-step instructions for building items like a grape vine arbor and a planting bench.

"We are both so passionate about gardening and growing our own food that we find ourselves talking to other people about it. Our influence both online and offline has inspired lots of people to try their hand at gardening—which is almost as cool as growing our own food in the first place."

Visit Shala and James Cross at their website, DoubleDanger.com.

The Cooperative Extension

The Cooperative Extension System is a national program whose prime directive is to educate people on a regional level in a wide array of areas from agriculture to economic development. Your local Extension Service is an invaluable resource for a variety of gardening and climate information that is specific to your area, offering everything from classes to advice, and even downloadable planting charts for your USDA Hardiness Zone.

In 1862, Congress created the land-grant system, which mandated that each state would have a university that would provide agricultural and mechanical education. A later act created research stations for the universities. The Extension Service was created in 1914, to bring the research results to the general public.

Are you wondering if your soil needs nutrients? You can send a sample to your Extension lab for testing. Costs and elements tested will vary by state, but the price is generally quite low, in the range of ten to twenty dollars. You will receive results telling you the soil texture, pH, salinity, amount of organic matter, and levels of nitrogen, potassium, phosphorus, zinc, iron, copper, manganese, and sulfur. The lab will also give you fertilizer and amendment suggestions based on these results, which can be incredibly valuable.

Do you wonder why the leaves are curling on your tree? See a strange bug in your yard? Have a general gardening question? You can call the Extension office for answers. You can also mail a sample of what you are trying to identify to the office.

Really got the gardening bug? They also offer you the opportunity to become certified as a Master Gardener.

To find contact information for your local Cooperative Extension office, visit www.csrees.usda.gov/Extension.

Moisture. It goes without saying (but we're going to say it anyway) that in order to be good for growing most things in the garden, soil needs to be able to retain a good amount of moisture while not staying soggy. Soil that has too much sand content, for example, will not retain much moisture content, while soil that is too high in clay may stay so wet that your plants may literally drown from a lack of airflow. How can you know the moisture level of your existing soil? Believe it or not, the process used by many soil labs to test your soil's moisture content is so simple that you can do it at home, though it really isn't necessary. The exact measurements involved are the stuff of scientific data, and most hobbyist gardeners will never have much of a reason to get into the nitty-gritty of their soil moisture.

To test the level of moisture in soil samples, the most common procedure in labs involves weighing your starting sample then putting it in the oven at 225°F (107°C) for 24 hours to remove all traces of moisture. After the sample is thoroughly dry, weighing it again on the same

(Above) Photos by Ric Deliantoni.

scale gives an accurate measurement of the true weight of the soil, and simple math will yield the moisture content of the sample.

What Kind of Soil Do I Have? Let's cut to the chase here and answer the question that is no doubt bugging you to death: What kind of soil do I have? For the most part, this is going to be an easy one to answer because there are three basic types of soil: sand, silt, and clay. What if you have soil that doesn't really look much like any of those and you want to know how your dirt stacks up? That's when you need a truly scientific method that involves a mayonnaise jar.

Starting with a clean jar, fill it about two-thirds full of water. Now add about a cup worth of soil. You want the jar to be nearly full between the water and the soil sample. Secure the lid on the jar tightly and shake the jar vigorously until all of the particles in the soil sample have been suspended in the water. Place the jar on a flat surface and wait 60 seconds. Using a marker, draw a line on the jar at the top of the layer of settled matter. This is the sand layer.

Leave the jar where it will be undisturbed and wait 60 minutes. There will be another layer atop the sand layer; mark it in the same way. This is the silt layer. Now leave the jar undisturbed for 24 hours and then return. Again, place a mark at the top of the settled soil. This is the third and final layer, the clay layer. Now you can look at the distance between the layers and make an educated guess as to how equally divided your soil is among the three layers.

Solving Soil Issues. Now that you know what soil type you are dealing with, you need to know what to do to make it right, right? Well, that's sort of right, in that you will need to correct soil issues if you plan to use the ground soil itself. The problem here lies in the time factor; you cannot transform clay soil into lush, fertile soil

Lasagna Gardening

Because it is easy and relatively painless, one method that we recommend for urban gardens is the process called lasagna gardening.

No, we are not talking about growing tomatoes, oregano, and basil together (though you can and should!). Lasagna gardening is a bed-preparation technique that requires no tilling or digging. You won't need a separate compost bin either, and it can even be used in your containers. The name *lasagna garden* refers to the layering technique used to build up the bed.

First, you select the area where you want to construct the bed. Sod or weeds in the way? No worries—you don't have to remove them. Now spread a thick layer of a degradable paper such as newspaper or cardboard over the plot to act as a mulch. This layer will kill any grass or weeds underneath.

Follow this with a layer of peat moss or coir (coconut fibers), about 2"–3" (5cm–8cm) thick. After this comes a layer of organic material 4"–6" (10cm–15cm) thick. You want to have a mixture of carbon-rich matter and nitrogen-rich matter, at about a 25-to-1 ratio. Common carbon-rich materials include leaves, newspaper, cardboard pieces, and dryer lint. For nitrogen, use grass clippings, algae, noninvasive weeds, and manure.

Continue layering between peat/coir and organic materials until the entire plot is 18"–24" (46cm–61cm) high. After this is finished, you can leave it to start decomposing if you like, or you also can plant immediately. All you have to do is push the layers aside to plant and then re-cover the layers when finished. As the plants grow, the materials will decompose, producing nutrient-rich compost for your plants.

If you want to make it decompose even faster, add some earthworms. You can also buy special composting worms from garden supply stores and websites.

Lasagna gardening is a great way for those with limited space to create rich soil.

(Above) Photos by Reggie Solomon.

overnight. It takes a year or more to balance a soil that is too heavy in clay or sand. We know what you are thinking: "I don't have a year! I want to grow right now!" The good news is that there is a way.

By building a raised bed over the area you want to plant, you can then backfill the raised area itself with a good soil blend that is ready-made for garden growing. This will save you a lot of time, and by using raised beds, you won't even need to dig up or otherwise till the existing earth. The simplest of raised beds can be easily constructed in just a couple of hours using sturdy four-by-four posts and untreated two-by-fours. Be absolutely sure you're using untreated wood because the chemicals used in treating some wood products can be highly toxic!

When to Start Preparing the Garden

Now that you have a better understanding of the soil in your garden, you need to look at the mechanics of preparing the garden for planting. The first step is to decide when to begin prep work, and that can depend largely on the area in which you live. By consulting the USDA Hardiness Zone Map, you will know your planting zone, and contacting your nearest branch of the Cooperative Extension will, in most cases, yield information on projected dates for planting various vegetables and fruits in your region.

Armed with this knowledge, you can begin prepping the garden area by digging, raking, or otherwise turning and loosening the soil in your garden beds. You'll want to do this about two weeks prior to planting to give yourself

plenty of time to properly aerate the soil, especially if this is the first time it is being planted. Amendments to the soil may be called for based on the soil type, texture, and pH.

Raised Beds

Raised bed gardening is becoming increasingly popular in urban areas and with good reason. You don't have to rely on the existing soil to be in good shape because you will fill a raised bed with the type and quality of soil that you choose. Raised beds can be constructed of many materials, but the most common is lumber.

Selecting Lumber for the Raised Bed. When selecting lumber for the construction of your raised bed, we recommend that you use untreated lumber. Though companies have not treated lumber with arsenic since around 2003, most lumber is still treated with a copper compound that can leech into the soil, leaving the potential for absorption into your food plants. For years, one popular raised bed component was discarded railroad ties, but under no circumstances should you use them anywhere near plants that will be used for food because they contain the highly toxic chemical creosote. If you are planting a purely visual garden, use the lumber of your choice, but if anything will be eaten, untreated lumber is the way to go.

Constructing a Raised Bed. This is definitely a point when your Garden Evaluation Worksheet from chapter 8 will prove to be quite handy. If you have used it, you have most certainly sketched out the basic layout for your raised beds, and using the grid as a scale model drawing, you will have ready-made notes for your trip to the lumber yard. Although your available space will dictate the size of your

Deciphering the Latin Botanical Names of Plants

From UrbanGardenCasual.com.

After you start venturing into the wonderful world of urban gardening, you may notice that plants can be called by many different names. In fact, every plant has at least two names—a common name and a botanical name in Latin.

Why would you want to learn the Latin name of a plant?

The Latin name of each plant is determined using a system called binomial nomenclature, invented in the 1700s by Swedish botanist Carl Linnaeus. This system gives each plant a specific two-part name comprised of the genus and the species. (It is also used to name animals.) The **genus** refers to a group of plants with similar characteristics. The **species** refers to one specific plant.

One advantage to knowing the Latin name is that you can make sure that you are talking about the right plant with other gardeners. Common names can vary by state, region, and even by family. But while a plant may have several common names, the Latin botanical name (with only a few isolated exceptions) will remain constant throughout the world.

Urban Garden Casual team member Vanessa Richins was once asked how to get rid of a "puncture vine." She had never heard of a plant by that name, and it wasn't until she saw the weed firsthand that she recognized it as a plant known to her as "goat heads." This common misunderstanding could have been avoided if the Latin botanical name *Tribulus terrestris* had been used. No matter what language someone speaks, the same Latin name is used by all.

Another fun characteristic of Latin names is that they can tell you something about the plant. If the species name is *Grandiflora,* for example, then you know that the plant has large (grandi-) flowers (-flora).

Even more fun is when botanists infuse humor or personal preferences when choosing the names for their plant discoveries. One tropical plant is *Macrocarpaea dies-viridis. Dies-viridis* literally means "green day" and in this case, the botanist happened to name the plant in honor of a favorite band. In the animal world, *Preseucoila imallshookupis* is a wasp that was named for Elvis Presley. Yes, really.

raised beds, it is generally a good rule of thumb to make them at least 8" (20cm) high, preferably no less than 1' (30cm) high to allow for proper root development. It isn't recommended for a raised bed to exceed 3' (1m) in height or 4' (1.2m) in width. Any taller or wider and it may be difficult to reach the entire bed. Smaller raised beds can be

tip **Save yourself time and hassle by having your lumber cut to size when you buy it. Most lumber retailers offer this service.**

What to Look For in a Fertilizer

From UrbanGardenCasual.com.

If you've ever stopped to look at the fertilizer shelf at the garden center, you may have wondered what the three numbers on the front of the packages represent. You'll typically see a series of three numbers separated by dashes, like 5-10-10.

These three numbers indicate the percentage of nitrogen, phosphorus, and potassium (abbreviated as N-P-K) that are contained in that bag.

For example, a 100-pound (45kg) bag of this 5-10-10 mix would have 5 pounds (2kg) nitrogen, 10 pounds (5kg) of phosphorus, and 10 pounds (5kg) of potassium. The remaining contents of the bag are composed of additional nutrients and fillers that make it easier for you to spread the fertilizer.

Nitrogen contributes to good stem and leaf growth. Lawns are especially fond of nitrogen. One sign that your plants may be nitrogen deficient is if the leaves begin to turn yellow.

Phosphorus helps in the production of flowers and fruits, so it is especially important for your vegetable and fruit plants. It also helps the plant strengthen its roots and resist diseases. If your plants need phosphorous, the leaves may start turning blue-green or purple.

Potassium helps plants develop disease and cold resistance, as well as aid in stem development. When a plant isn't getting enough potassium, the veins on the leaves may start turning yellow, while the leaf tips turn brown and start curling.

For your vegetables, a good general recommendation is to pick a fertilizer that has a ratio of 1-2-1 or 1-2-2. You can figure this ratio yourself by dividing the numbers on your fertilizer to the lowest common denominator. We don't like math either, but this one is really simple. Our 5-10-10 fertilizer would fit this. When you divide each number by 5 the resulting ratio is 1-2-2.

built using a basic two-by-four construction, where the joints are either screwed together or nailed in place with metal brackets available from your hardware store. It is recommended that you bury four-by-four posts at least 1' (30cm) deep in each corner of the raised bed. This will ensure the bed's stability and give you something to secure the lumber to.

Before you begin construction, ensure the area on which you are working is level. Use a level, which is an inexpensive tool that you will find handy in a variety of applications. As you are laying out each piece of lumber for your raised bed, check to make sure it is level before securing it permanently to the corner posts.

If you find your raised bed area to be uneven, there are several methods by which you might level things out. If the grade is off by only a few inches or less, a shovel and leveling sand (which is basically fine sand) can be used to create a level surface. In a more severe situation, it may be necessary to build up the ground level by using a combination of dirt, sand, and lengths of lumber to act as shims of a sort.

If you choose to paint or stain your raised beds, we recommend

(Above) Photo by Ric Deliantoni.

the use of an environmentally aware product with lower VOCs, or volatile organic compounds, that can have a negative impact on air quality. Look for good quality sealing products made from a base of either soy or whey, both of which can be used with excellent results and a minimal impact on the environment or your food.

Buying Seedlings

Seedlings are at the center of every garden, and yet when preparing for our growing seasons, we often don't take them into much consideration at all. Although seedlings are a necessary part of the gardening process, many folks think they can just stop at a nearby warehouse store and make their selections. It seems a bit counterintuitive to go through the time, effort, and expense of starting an urban garden only to allow the plants you include to be an afterthought.

One of the biggest stumbling blocks for people who are new to gardening is that they neglect to plan ahead. We often tell new gardeners that one of the best ways to ensure a good crop is to already be working on the next season's plants as soon as this season's choices are established. Sound crazy? Sure, but not too many gardening-types claim to be sane. No matter what your level of plant experience, planning ahead is very important.

Your local Extension Service office will have information on the ideal dates for planting various fruits and vegetables. Any specific questions about planting dates can be directed to them, but the annual chart that most offices produce will be a great starting point for planning your seedlings.

Comparing Seed Catalogs

How do seed catalogs and seed magazines (also referred to as "garden porn" by some especially avid readers) stack up against each other in helping gardeners plan and decide what to grow in their gardens? Most gardeners don't have to worry about quality when purchasing seeds and plants from major providers, so what largely distinguishes providers is how helpful they are to gardeners in planning and preparing their gardens.

Here are some things to look for when selecting a seed catalog:

Organization

Catalogs can be organized in a few ways.

Visually. Catalogs organized in a visual manner are beautiful to look at. Their large full-color spreads of juicy vegetables are organized to maximize visual appeal. On one double-page spread, you'll find radishes, flowers, and tomatoes all profiled together, not because of their varietal or gardening relation, but because the colors are visually pleasing in juxtaposition from a layout perspective.

This method of organization, while certainly visually appealing at first, can wear on you as you compare products from different catalogs and get closer to actually ordering because the catalog is not organized by category, which can make it difficult to quickly find what you are looking for.

Categorically. Just like it sounds—everything is organized by category. Each plant has its own section, making it quick and easy to find a specific variety and compare it to another catalog. What these catalogs lack in beauty, they make up for in functionality.

Visual Categories. Don't assume that if a catalog is pretty it will be a nightmare to navigate. Some are well organized and beautifully photographed—the best of both worlds. You should be able to tell pretty quickly if a catalog is organized in a style that will work well for you.

Content

Catalogs are used to sell products, so be prepared for some glowing descriptions. Flowery descriptions sparse on technical gobbledegook impart the feeling that you can easily and successfully grow anything simply by buying a packet of seeds. These catalogs are light on technical information, most likely because these additional details might frighten the average consumer.

There is, however, some vital information that even novices will benefit from knowing, specifically the estimated days to maturity. Estimated days to maturity is especially important to gardeners with short growing seasons. As an urban gardener, having the option to choose seeds with shorter growing periods is advantageous because a variety of environmental factors, such as shadows cast by neighboring buildings, can effectively shorten the growing season and lengthen the time needed to grow some vegetables.

In-depth catalogs include growing information that describes the plant and the best way to grow and harvest it. They also may have a key code directory that notes which vegetables are heirloom, cold tolerant, easy choice for gardening, organic, and hybrid, and even a section that compares seed and plant types with each other so you'll know which seed minimizes or maximizes a feature you may find more or less desirable.

Selection

Some catalogs specialize in mainstream plants that appeal to basic gardeners. If you're looking for a standard selection, mainstream catalogs will meet your needs.

Others appeal to serious gardeners and even farmers, selling seed by the packet and by the pound. These types of catalogs will offer more selection and varieties and go beyond the standard plants.

Others appeal to the organic crowd. Although organic seed production may limit the number of seed varieties offered, it certainly doesn't limit the rarity and uniqueness of their offerings.

Explore multiple options before you purchase your seeds. A wealth of products and information are available online and in catalogs.

(Below) Photo by Reggie Solomon.

Finding Seedlings

While living in the city can be the ultimate in convenience, some areas have yet to jump on the urban gardening bandwagon. You may be able to find top-notch takeout at 2 a.m., but finding a well-stocked garden center? Not so much. The good news for those who live in these areas is that you can be a trendsetter, while the bad news is that finding much in the way of seedling selection is going to be a challenge. In this section, we discuss a few options for finding the seedlings that are right for you.

The DIY Option—Grow Your Own

We would be remiss if we did not first suggest that to get the best seedlings around, you need only look to your own windowsill. That's right, folks—growing your own plants

from seed is the least expensive and easiest way to be sure that you can grow exactly what you want. Because seeds are available via the Internet and mail-order companies, you are no longer restrained by the meager offerings at your local superstore.

For step-by-step instructions on how to grow your own seedlings from seed, check out chapter 5.

Mom and Pop Know Best

An important and often ignored part of the gardening resurgence in recent years is the emphasis that it puts on *eating local*. By consuming foods and products that are produced closer to where you live, you are reducing the carbon emissions necessary to get that food to your plate, thus helping the environment. In environmental circles, this concept is known as *food miles* and the fewer the food miles, the better.

The very same premise applies to where you shop. Whenever possible, we want to encourage you to buy locally produced items from locally owned businesses. If there is a local mom-and-pop garden shop or nursery in your neighborhood, you owe it to yourself and to your community to stop in and check out what they have to offer. In many cases, they will offer hard-to-find varieties of seedlings that big-box stores just can't match. You might pay a bit more for them, but it will be worth it.

Know Thy Neighbor

How well do you know your neighbors? One of the downfalls to urban living is that we get so busy and caught up in our own lives that we forget to reach out and connect with those around us. Talk to your neighbors, friends, or those who you see tending plants on their front stoops.

Chances are you have friends or neighbors who are growing their own seedlings at home. If you're good, you might be able to talk them into growing a couple for you as well. Even if they don't grow their own seedlings at home, your neighbors are most often the single best source for information on where to get the goods, so get outside and meet them.

Not sure how to meet like-minded garden folk? You could always look for the telltale dirt under the fingernails, but one of the best conversation starters in the world is for you to show an appreciation for someone's handiwork. See a nice window box or hanging planter full of cherry tomatoes on your street? Strike up a conversation with the gardener, and you will likely have a new friend for life.

The Internet to the Rescue

You shop for shoes, clothes, accessories, and even pizza online. Doesn't it make sense that you can shop for garden seedlings there, too? In reality, just about anything that you might want for your garden is available on the Internet, including seed varieties that you won't find in your local stores. Whether you are using the Internet to shop or simply to research the plants you want to grow, it is an amazing resource for urban gardeners all over the world.

For a list of some of our favorite online garden shops, check out chapter 8.

Garden Centers and Big-Box Stores

While it may appear that we have a vendetta against big-box stores and large garden centers, that simply is not the case. In the urban environment, a large portion of the population simply does not own a car, so trekking down to the big superstore involves planning, public transportation,

and being able to carry everything you purchased. When was the last time that you went to a garden center and could carry all of your purchases in one trip?

That said, depending on your location, it may be necessary—or you may simply prefer—to do your garden shopping at one of these larger stores. There is nothing wrong with that at all, so long as you have the means to get your purchases from point A (store) to point B (home). In years past in New York City, there were dedicated regular weekend bus trips to the outskirts of town where a popular Swedish home furnishings store was located. The cargo area would be packed full of the shoppers' wares, helping to make the trip a little less cumbersome. It is possible that such trips exist in your area, so check around.

Wrap It Up

In this chapter, you learned how to get started and really get your hands dirty in your new urban garden. We talked about the how-to of prepping the garden area, as well as understanding the different types of and components of soil. We also looked at constructing raised garden beds and how they can be beneficial in areas that don't have the most plant-friendly soil compositions. Finally, we investigated your options for seedlings and how to find them.

In the next chapter, we're going to dig even deeper and learn how to grow what we've got. Grab your favorite beverage, turn on some music, and let's go!

5 How to Grow It

One of the most common rookie mistakes we have seen first-time gardeners make is that they take on too much at once. We're not going to say that gardening is an easy thing to do, and anyone who does say this is either completely delusional or just plain lying. Gardening is not easy. There, we said it.

When you are just getting your gardening feet wet, you should resist the urge to overcommit yourself by overplanting. Start small for the first season with just a few plants that you know you will be able to manage. This will give you a much better frame of reference for how much work is involved in the care and maintenance of your garden, and it will better equip you to deal with larger numbers of plants in the future. Select a core group of plants that you feature often in your favorite or frequently prepared dishes, and you will be rewarded with fresh produce that will impress everyone.

One great beginner garden is the least complicated as well. Try your hand at a salsa garden, and you'll be wowing your family and friends with home-grown tomatoes, peppers, onions, and cilantro for months. Many varieties of these plants do

Give the Gift of Gardening

Want a unique gift that will not soon be forgotten? Why not give the gift of a salad garden?

Here's what you'll need to make your own salad garden in a box:

- An oblong planter box (the ones we have are plastic)
- A mixture of potting soil and manure (both available at any good nursery or garden center). A ratio of 3-to-1 is a good starting point.
- Seeds (a combination of seeds like butter lettuce, red leaf lettuce, mustard, arugula, Swiss chard, carrots, radishes)

Fill the planter with the soil/manure mix. Smooth the top, divide the space into sections and plant one type of seed in each section. As the various types of seeds germinate, you can thin them and eat the thinnings in a salad. As the plants continue to grow, cut enough leaves to make a salad.

The young radish and carrot leaves will be a tasty addition to salad, and later you can allow them to mature and eat the carrots and radishes. This is a gift that will please anyone all summer long!

Profiles in Casual: Meg Graustein

(Left) Photo by Meg Graustein.

Location: New Haven, Connecticut
USDA Hardiness Zone: 6

New Haven, Connecticut, native Meg Graustein transformed her front lawn along a quiet city street into the ultimate urban garden. An increasing number of people are moving toward planting vegetables rather than grass in the front of their homes as a way to better use precious water resources.

Why did you decide to turn your front lawn into a vegetable garden, and how did your neighbors react?
I decided to rip out my front lawn (and a good portion of the back) for a few reasons. I missed living on a farm and having fresh produce. I eat a mostly vegan, gluten-free diet, so I eat a lot of vegetables, and I like knowing where my food comes from. And lastly, I love gardening and playing in the dirt.

The front yard has direct sun all day long, making it perfect for growing many vegetables. The garden is way less maintenance than a lawn, especially because I don't like mowing. During super hot and dry summers, lawns do require some water, but for gardens, it's water that is going into food to sustain me as opposed to water being used to keep a lawn pretty.

For me, there was never a question about ripping out the lawn to create a garden. To keep the amount of water use down, I mulch the veggies heavily in the summer. This year I'm installing rain barrels so I can use the run off from the roof to water the garden.

My neighbors seem to like it, or at least I haven't heard any negative comments. Whenever I'm working in the garden, people stop and ask questions and talk about their gardens or plans for gardens. I get a lot of questions about how to build raised beds.

Why did you choose raised bed gardening versus gardening directly in the ground?
Raised beds can produce higher yields of food per square foot than conventional in-ground gardening due to better drainage, which allows for improved root growth and an expanded growing season. There is less weeding involved in raised bed gardening, and it's easier to work in.

I also chose to use raised beds because the soil in the ground was not that great, and there was a fair amount of junk in it—old pottery, nails, glass. I used a mix of peat moss, vermiculite, and organic compost in the beds, and it has been incredibly productive. I really like the look of the raised beds, and when the growing season is over, there is still something interesting to look at—not just a big patch of dirt.

What vegetables have you found to be especially suited for raised bed gardening?

Carrots grow out of control! Apparently the combination of peat moss, vermiculite, and compost I used to fill the beds is perfectly suited for carrots. It is loose enough and has enough nutrients that carrots thrive. A couple of years ago, I got more than forty eggplants from one plant. I kept giving away eggplants to everyone who walked by. I haven't grown eggplant since.

I had watermelon and butternut squashes growing up the sides of my house. I had to cut them back because they almost ripped the phone line off the side of the house. I grow as much as possible up trellises so I can plant closer together. I plant lettuces and other greens under or behind the trellises so they get some shade, and it seems to work well.

Green, leafy vegetables have absolutely flourished in the raised beds. I haven't found anything that doesn't do well. I grow potatoes in cages and have gotten huge yields. Everything seems to thrive in the raised beds, and they are so easy to plant and work in.

quite well in containers and are very simple to maintain, so with just a little time, you are almost guaranteed to be a success.

Starting Seeds

Nearly every gardener has, at some point, tried to start his or her garden from seed at least once. For some of us, growing from seed is the only way to go, while others enjoy the hassle-free approach of stopping by the nursery or garden center and picking up a few seedlings that are ready to transplant. You may remember being in elementary school and growing some random vegetable plant from a seed planted in a milk carton as part of a class project. In much the same way, today's gardeners with small children often find that starting seeds is a great opportunity to share gardening with the family and to increase interest in the entire process among their youngsters.

There are a lot of things to know about starting seeds, but the basics are pretty simple:

1. Seeds need moisture and warmth to germinate.
2. After they germinate, seedlings need nutrients, warmth, and light to grow.

Seed-Starting Kits

For those readers who would like to try starting their garden seeds without the hassle of buying a lot of individual items, several companies produce complete seed-starting kits. This is one of the simplest methods for seed starting that we have found. All you have to add are seeds and water. Although there are several kits and manufacturers

(Left) Photo by Ric Deliantoni.

to choose from, we recommend those produced by the Jiffy company, which also owns the popular seed company Ferry-Morse.

For new gardeners who aren't quite sure just how involved and invested they want to be, Jiffy makes a mini greenhouse product that comes complete with twelve dehydrated peat seed-starting pods and a plastic container with a lid. To get started, you simply rehydrate the pellets by adding water. When the pellets have absorbed all the water they can, you plant the seeds carefully into each individual pod by first poking a small indention into the top of the pellet with a leftover chopstick from last week's Chinese takeout. Once the pellets have been seeded, you simply attach the plastic greenhouse lid and place it in a warm place until the seeds sprout (see seed packaging for approximate germination times).

Potting Up

When seedlings have grown their second set of leaves (the *true leaves*), it is time to pot them up into a seedling pot. A seedling pot will most often be in the 3" to 4" (8cm to 10cm) size range. You have plenty of options for these pots, ranging from the familiar plastic ones to those made of natural and biodegradable fibers. What you use depends on your personal taste, of course, but the obvious benefit to using the fiber pots is that when you are ready to transplant them either into a larger container or into the ground outdoors, you only have to tear away the bottom of the pot and you can plant the entire thing, pot and all. If you opt for plastic pots, you may be able to save them for future use, but you will need to take steps to ensure they have been properly sanitized prior to reuse (see the sidebar on page 82).

Growing Salad Greens

Being able to have fresh salad greens on a moment's notice has to be one of the most fulfilling parts of growing your own urban garden. No last minute trips to the supermarket when you want a quick salad. All you have to do is pinch off a few leaves; your salad literally is at your fingertips! Even better is the fact that growing salad greens is one of the easiest gardening tasks, no matter what your level of previous experience.

(Right) Photo by Ric Deliantoni.

How Long Do Seeds Last?

Many gardeners store garden seeds—especially from vegetables—at the end of the growing season, but the seeds will not last forever. The natural shelf life of garden seeds depends on the kind of plant.

Store seeds in a cool, dry location so they will last longer than their natural shelf life. They can be placed in a sealed jar in the refrigerator with a moisture absorbent like rice, silica packets, or powdered milk.

One Year. Seeds that can be stored successfully for one year include parsnips, spinach and sweet corn. Annual flower seeds can last from one to three years.

Two Years. Beans, beets, parsley, peas, peppers and Swiss chard have a natural shelf life of two years. Leeks and onions can last two to three years. Perennial flower seeds are good for two to four years.

Three Years. A shelf life of three years can be expected for carrots, cucumbers, lettuce, melons, Oriental greens, rutabagas and tomatoes. Broccoli, brussels sprouts, cabbage, cauliflower, collard, kale and kohlrabi will last three to five years. Squash seeds can be planted for three to four years.

Four Years. Radish and turnip seeds can last up to four years.

Reusing Plastic Pots

Whenever we buy plants at a nursery or garden supply center, we are left with a stack of empty pots. It just doesn't seem right to toss them, and you don't have to. Provided you take a few precautions, these pots are perfectly fine to use again when you are potting up your plants or starting your own seeds at home.

Why are these precautions necessary? There are all sorts of bacteria, molds, and fungi that can be present in potting soil. There are even diseases that can be spread by reusing pots that haven't been properly sanitized.

Begin by rinsing away any visible dirt and debris from the pots and then give them a thorough hand washing. You can then wash them in the dishwasher using the sanitizer setting if you so desire. If not, you will need to take another step and use a sanitizing solution. We have seen references to sanitizing pots in a bleach solution, but that's just not the way we do things. No matter how you slice it, bleach is toxic, and we don't like using toxic chemicals where we are going to be growing food. Instead, we use a 1:1 solution of water and white vinegar.

Soak your clean pots in the vinegar-and-water solution for an hour and then allow them to air dry before reusing them. For terra cotta pots, you can even place them in an oven set at 225°F (107°C) for half an hour.

The Salad Table

If you have a paved space that is 3' × 5' (91cm × 152cm), you can build your own salad table and be able to enjoy fresh greens, even if you don't have the ground space to plant it traditionally. The table was created by Jon Traunfeld from the Maryland Cooperative Extension Service. Their website, extension.umd.edu, gives detailed instructions for building a salad table, as well as several ways you can modify it for different crops—using wider boards to grow beans and peppers, for example.

There are other benefits to building a salad table. Those with problems kneeling won't have to bend over much because the table is 4' (122cm) high. With the plants up off the ground, it's much less likely that rabbits and other garden pests will nibble on them. Don't have enough room for a full salad table? The site also includes instructions for making a smaller salad box.

What can you grow in a salad table or box?

- Lettuces and greens (all sorts—lettuces, endive, escarole, mustard greens, arugula, kale, cress, broccoli rabe, mizuna, and more)
- Radishes
- Spinach
- Chard
- Beets
- Herbs (e.g., parsley, cilantro, basil, and thyme)

From the basic design, you can choose to be as simple or creative as you like. We have seen salad tables that were nothing more than the two-by-four frame and others that were finished with a variety of decorative accents. How will *your* salad table grow?

(Right) Photo by Ric Deliantoni.

Growing Herbs

If you are entirely new to gardening
and want a fairly simple way to make
a grand entrance into the pastime, an
herb garden may be just the thing for
you. For the most part, herbs are prolific, easy to grow, and generally quite
forgiving of those rookie mistakes
like watering too little or too much.
The most important suggestion
when selecting herbs to grow is one
that should be obvious—grow what
you eat. At the end of the day, there is
nothing like a nice mojito (recipe in
chapter 7) made with fresh mint that
you grew yourself.

tip When growing herbs in
containers, experiment
with different options for grouping different herbs together
depending on how you use them.
Sage, thyme, and oregano are
excellent companions in a soup
pot, and they grow well together.
Try growing a trio of different
types of basil or mint together
and have fun with the different
flavors in your favorite dishes!

(Above) Photo by www.sustainableecho.com.

HERB CHART

Plant	Sunlight Needs	Spacing	Plant Size	Type	Container
Basil	full sun	12" (30cm)	24"+ (61cm+)	annual	yes
Chives	full sun	bunches	8"–12" (20cm–30cm)	perennial	yes
Dill	full sun	9" (23cm)	36"+ (91cm+)	annual	yes
Fennel	full sun	12" (30cm)	24"+ (61cm+)	annual	yes
Lavender	partial sun	varies	varies	perennial	yes
Lemon balm	partial sun	12" (30cm)	24" (61cm)	perennial	yes
Marjoram	full sun	12" (30cm)	6"–12" (15cm–30cm)	annual	yes
Mint family	partial sun	varies	varies	both	yes
Oregano	full sun	12"–24" (30cm–61cm)	12" (30cm)	perennial	yes
Parsley	full sun	8" (20cm)	8"–12" (20cm–30cm)	annual	yes
Rosemary	full sun	12"–24" (30cm–61cm)	12"–36"+ (30cm–91cm+)	annual	yes
Sage	full sun	15"–18" (38cm–46cm)	18"–24" (46cm–61cm)	perennial	yes
Thyme	full sun	3"–10" (8cm–25cm)	4"– 8" (10cm–20cm)	perennial	yes

(Above) Photo by Ric Deliantoni.

One of the biggest problems we hear about when beginning gardeners work with herbs is that the seeds are so tiny they're nearly impossible to work with. This usually leads to using too many seeds in too small of a space. One of the most creative and ingenious methods for dealing with this frustration is through the use of a process called "seed taping." It is exactly what it sounds like—affixing seeds to a thin strip of paper that will dissolve into the earth, making it easier to put seeds exactly where you want them. Although seed tapes can be purchased at many gardening stores, they can be really expensive.

Make Your Own Seed Tape

If you have never heard of seed tape, chances are you will need this section more than you could have imagined, especially if you want to grow some of the more tiny-seeded garden wonders like radishes or carrots. For years, many of us have struggled with magnifying glasses, tweezers, and other equally cumbersome methods to plant minute seeds in the right spot, only to be disappointed when we had too few (or too many) seeds starting in the wrong place. When you use seed tape, you never have to worry about that problem again.

To make your own seed tape, gather the following:

- Seeds
- A roll of cheap toilet paper (the cheaper the better)
- Washable white nontoxic school glue or a simple flour-water mixture

Did you know that popular herbs coriander and cilantro come from the same plant? The leaves are cilantro while the seeds are coriander.

Growing Carrots

Carrots are a cool-season vegetable. They can be planted in the spring as soon as the ground has thawed. You can also plant a second crop in the fall. The best growth happens when the temperature is between 60°F–70°F (16°C–21°C). If it is too hot, growth will slow, and the roots will become coarse and develop a bad flavor. If it is too cool, the roots will be too thin and long.

Start with well-drained soil. There shouldn't be any stones or clods, and it needs to be loose. Carrots are the roots of the plant—if they encounter rocks or other hard items, the roots may curve, fork or both! The soil also needs to be fairly deep so the roots have room to grow. You can use a container as long as it is at least 12" (30cm) deep.

Plant seeds ¼" (6mm) deep in rows that are 1"–1½" (3cm–4cm) apart. You can plant seeds every three weeks until early July if you would like to have carrots throughout the entire growing season. As far as watering goes, carrots are not drought tolerant. Water thoroughly about once a

(Above) Photo by Ric Deliantoni.   (Above) Photo by Sarah D. Cady.

week. If you water less frequently but for longer periods, it will promote deeper root growth. This is especially beneficial for a root vegetable like carrots.

Harvesting the carrots is easy: Simply pull the plant out of the ground when the visible part of the root is ¾"–1½" (2cm–4cm) wide—sooner if you want baby carrots.

(Above) Photo by Ric Deliantoni.

- Toothpicks or chopsticks
- A ruler
- A pen

Generally speaking, three squares of toilet paper will measure 12" (30cm) in length and 4" (10cm) in width, which means that three three-square sections will make up a 1' (30cm) section. This is perfect for container and square-foot gardeners and makes planting tiny herb seeds and small row plants like carrots and radishes much simpler and quicker.

1. Lay out your toilet paper in the desired formation (we suggest a 12" × 12" [30cm × 30cm] square). Start by reading the seed packet, if available, to find out what the suggested spacing is between seeds. If you don't have instructions with spacing suggestions, check chapter 8 for info on where you can find what you need. Using a ruler and a pen, place a dot at the desired increments until you have covered the entire surface of the paper with dots.

2. Using a toothpick or chopstick, place a dab of glue or the flour-water mixture on each dot, working on one square of toilet paper at a time. Then place a seed on each drop of glue. You may find it helpful to pick up the seed with the same toothpick because the glue residue will help you pick up one at a time.

3. When the entire surface area is glued and seeded, allow it to dry thoroughly. On each section of paper, write what seeds it contains and then fold

your seed tape and slide it into a zipper bag and store it until you are ready to plant it.

To plant the seed tape, make sure your soil is smooth and free of debris and stones. Lay out the seed tape in the desired area and cover the tape by sprinkling it with soil. When covered with between ⅛" (3mm) and ¼" (6mm) of soil, lightly pat the soil and water. It will help to cover the soil with a piece of cardboard for the first few days until the sprouts begin to break the surface of the soil.

Now that the tape has begun to sprout, you can easily see which seeds on the tape did not come up. Give it enough time to be sure and then reseed the empty spaces. This ensures the best use of the space you have available.

Other Uses for Seed Tape. The use of seed tape makes seed starting so simple; why should we limit ourselves? If you are bold enough to start all of your urban garden veggies, herbs, and fruit from seed, using seed tape is one of the simplest and most foolproof ways to do it. Creating a seed tape is also an excellent way to get your kids involved and interested in the gardening process, and it is completely safe to do.

You can use seed tape to plant single rows of whatever you like by simply cutting the paper into a 1½" (4cm) wide strip that is the length you need and follow the rest of the instructions as listed. Just be certain to leave the required amount of space between the seeds or be prepared to thin them out later (and if you're to going take time to thin them out, why bother with seed tape in the first place?).

Growing Herbs in Containers

When growing herbs in containers, it is imperative that you select a container with adequate drainage. When starting herbs that will remain indoors, you can start herbs at any time of year, but when you plan to move them outdoors, it is a good rule of thumb to start the seeds in mid- to late February so they will be fully established and ready for their outdoor debut as soon as the last chance of frost has passed.

When selecting an area to be home for your herbs, bear in mind that they will need a minimum of five hours of sunlight per day. This makes southern and western exposures good for many herb gardens, and even if you are growing indoors, windows that face south or west are generally the best choice. One idea you may not have considered if you are planning to grow your herbs indoors is to look for a decorative window box just like the type you'd see hanging on the outside of a window. If you have a deep window ledge inside, these boxes can be a great option that is both utilitarian and original at the same time.

tip Pressed for space but still want a variety of fresh herbs at your fingertips? Look no further than a strawberry pot to grow an array of herbs with similar needs, and you will be rewarded with beautiful and delicious herbs for months!

Try a combination of oregano, thyme, savory, chives, and sage for a surefire winner. These herbs have similar needs as far as light and water, and they complement each other very well in a stew pot!

Growing Garlic in a Container

Members of the allium family are all well suited for container growing, and garlic is an especially useful plant to grow in a small garden space. Not only are the garlic bulbs easy to grow, the greens can be harvested and eaten once before allowing them to finish growing. They are delicious and a very healthy addition to stir-frys or salads.

The most important thing to remember about garlic is that it is absolutely essential to grow it in well-drained soil. If the soil in your container becomes waterlogged, the garlic will rot and will not grow. So make sure to use potting soil specifically designed for container growing.

Line the bottom of your planter with a few handfuls of pea gravel or small stones. This will ensure good drainage. Then fill a deep container with potting soil. Add in a few handfuls of manure and mix well. Allow at least 10"

(25cm) for growth because garlic and other alliums need a medium-deep pot.

Large pots that are about 18" (46cm) deep and 24" (61cm) across are a great option. A long, square window box type of planter would be good, too, as long as it is at least 8" (20cm) deep.

Plant one clove of garlic 2" (5cm) deep, with the pointy end pointing up, and leave at least 5" (13cm) between cloves. It's better to plant fewer per container because

Studies have shown that children who learn to grow their own vegetables are more likely to eat them.

crowding them will cause your production to fall. Give them lots of room and they will reward you!

Water in the bulbs after you plant them. Place the container in the sunniest location in your garden or on your porch. Water them only when the soil seems dry—do not overwater.

In the spring, the greens will shoot up quickly. You can harvest the first batch of young greens to eat in a salad or stir-fry. After that, leave the greens alone. However, if the plants begin to flower, cut the flower so the plant will focus on growing more bulbs. Your garlic will be ready to harvest when the green shoots turn brown and wilt. Garlic can be stored in a cool dry place for a month or two.

Growing Tomatoes

Tomatoes are easily one of the most popular garden plants grown in the United States, and with good reason—tomatoes are everywhere! From burgers to salsa, pasta sauce to chili, it is tough to imagine going too long without a tomato on your plate in one form or another. Growing tomatoes is a great alternative to paying top dollar at the supermarket

Radiator Charlie's Mortgage Lifter Tomato

The beauty of heirloom tomatoes reaches far beyond the dinner table and into history itself. They are a breath of fresh air that foster family and friendship in today's world of genetically mutated plants.

Heirloom seeds are truly by the people, for the people. They are not mass manufactured and sold in every store, instead being handed down by generations of real people who value taste and purity over appearance.

In the early 1940s, a man without any formal education who went by the name of "Radiator Charlie" decided that he wanted to create a better tomato. He started with the largest seeds he could find and planted them in circles with a plant in the center.

With the careful precision of a scientist, he would collect pollen from the plants (in a baby's ear syringe, no less) and deposit it on the center plant—the plump, pink German Johnson variety of tomato.

Seven years later, Charlie was happy with the result and never worked with any other plant variety, tomato or otherwise. As it turned out, he wouldn't need to. The new variety that he created would garner coverage in the local news media when they caught wind of the plants that could regularly produce delicious tomatoes that weighed more than a pound each, often as much as 2 or 3 pounds.

Radiator Charlie would go on to grow and sell his seedlings for one dollar each—big money at the time. The money he made turned out to be enough to pay off the mortgage on his modest six-thousand-dollar home, and thus the tomato got its moniker and Radiator Charlie's Mortgage Lifter was born.

(Above) Photo by Reggie Solomon.

(Left) Photo by Reggie Solomon.

for tasteless tomatoes that were picked in a hothouse while they were still green and then treated with ethylene gas to make them turn red.

First, let's take a quick look at some basic information you need to know about tomatoes before you choose which type to grow.

There are two classifications for tomatoes—determinate and indeterminate. The class you choose can and will affect your overall yield, but you should base your decision on the amount of time and effort you want to dedicate to your tomato plants.

Determinate Tomatoes

A determinate tomato plant produces its entire crop at once. This can be both a blessing and a curse, depending on how prepared you are to deal with a sudden influx of ripe fruit. Still, determinate tomato plants can be good for first-timers who don't want to deal with a long growing season.

Indeterminate Tomatoes

Indeterminate tomato plants produce throughout the growing season, often right up to the first frost of fall. The yield is generally considerably higher, so preparation is necessary beforehand. In other words, you will need to have a plan for all the tomatoes.

Hybrids or Heirlooms

The field of tomato plants is separated into two basic types. These are two entirely different types of plants that are each valuable in their own right. Both hybrid and heirloom tomato varieties are popular and for all sorts of reasons.

The Great Debate: Stakes or Cages?

It has been the cause of much heated debate among gardeners: Should you use stakes or cages for your maturing tomato plants? Different schools of thought will laud the benefits of one over the other, but by and large, it is a matter of personal preference. When growing larger beefsteak varieties such as Radiator Charlie's Mortgage Lifter, our recommendation is to use strong and sturdy cages because each fruit can weigh as much as 3 pounds (1.4kg) or more, and you will be thankful for the added support down the road. Pot-bound tomatoes are often just as well served with careful staking, but if you do plan on staking your tomatoes, you should plan to do so when you transplant the seedling into its final pot because inserting a stake any later may damage the plant's root system.

(Above) Photo by Reggie Solomon.

Hybrids. Hybrid tomato plants are those that have been genetically modified to produce consistent fruit that meets varying sets of criteria. Tomato plants have been hybrid-ized for size, color, flavor, consistency, and yield, as well as being tailor-made to grow in a wide array of climates and situations. Want to grow tomatoes in a hanging planter on your front porch in Texas? There's a hybrid for you.

Some of our favorite hybrid tomato varieties include:

- Big Beef
- Brandy Boy
- Mexicana
- Sun Gold

Heirlooms. Heirloom tomato plants are rich in history. Unlike hybrids, heirloom are not genetically modified in a lab and, as a result, the fruit can often be considered 'ugly', with odd shapes making them appear deformed. Rest assured that while these tomatoes may look odd to you, the flavor will more than make up for it.

When it comes to heirloom tomatoes, nearly all are favorites, but there are definitely some varieties that deserve honorable mentions:

- Aunt Ruby's German Green
- Extreme Bush
- San Marzano
- Silvery Fir Tree
- Radiator Charlie's Mortgage Lifter
- Rutgers

Which do you choose? When it comes down to an issue of sustainability, the heirloom tomato is the only way to go. The seeds in hybrid tomatoes are largely sterile, making the seed-saving process a fruitless effort (pardon the pun). Even the seeds that have not been sterilized will rarely produce true from seed. Heirloom tomato seeds, on the other hand, are easily collected, stored, and planted season after season with great results.

(Above) Photo by Ric Deliantoni.

(Above) Photo by Susy Morris, chiotsrun.com.

How to Grow Tomatoes

If you plan to start your tomatoes from seed, you will need to get started about two months before the last frost in your area. Tomatoes require a lot of time to grow, so it is almost always better to start the seeds indoors. You will want to sow seeds in a good-quality, seed-starting medium, and if you are growing more than one type of tomato, be sure to clearly label your rows. Here is a general timeline for what to expect:

Day 1. Sow seeds about ¼" (6mm) deep and ½" (1mm) apart. A good way for beginners to gauge the correct depth is to use a regular pencil. Instead of digging a row out of the seed-starting medium, simply press the pencil lengthwise into the starter with just enough pressure to create an indention about the same depth as the pencil itself. Place the seeds in these indentions. Sprinkle enough additional seed-starter mix to fill the trenches and cover the new seeds, and water thoroughly but lightly with a plant mister. Cover the tray with plastic wrap and set it in a warm place that will remain a consistent temperature of no less than 75°F (24°C). A good light source is important.

Day 7. By now, most of your seeds will have germinated. If you are growing more than one variety, you will be thankful that you heeded our advice and labeled them. Why? Because the first leaves or *cotyledon* leaves all look alike, and it may take months before you can differentiate

tip Urban Garden Casual gardeners have found that a fork is perfect for gently loosening new seedlings from their starting medium. The fork can be used to lift the new seedling and its fragile root system into a new pot with minimal damage.

between tomato varieties (in some cases, you may never be able to tell). Remove the plastic wrap covering when the seeds begin to germinate.

Day 15. All of your seedlings have germinated, and the cotyledon leaves are a vibrant green, indicating that they have enough light, warmth and moisture.

Day 30. New leaves are beginning to appear. These are known as the first *true* leaves, and they indicate that the seedling is ready to be pricked out. Pricking out the seedling is nothing more than carefully removing each tiny seedling from its starter tray and potting it up into its own 3"–4" (8cm–10cm) starter pot that you have filled with a good-quality starter soil. When you do prick out your tomatoes, always hold them by the cotyledon leaves and never by the stem. Bury the seedling all the way up to the base of the cotyledon leaves.

One thing to keep in mind when potting up tomato seedlings (and likewise when you are planting them either in the ground or into the final pot that will be their home for the season) is that the deeper you plant a tomato seedling, the stronger the plant will be. It is common practice,

Tomato Foes

From TomatoCasual.com.

(Left) Photo by Howard Walfish.

As there are plants that cohabitate well with tomatoes, there are likewise those that should be avoided at all costs. Let's take a quick look at a few plants your tomatoes want to stay away from and why:

Corn and tomatoes share a common enemy, though it might confuse some because it is known by two different names. The corn earworm or tomato fruitworm does not discriminate, and it is a bad, bad thing. These miniature monsters are generally between 1½" (4cm) and 2" (5cm) long, and they live to make a meal of your tomatoes, corn, and lots of other plants. Planting corn and tomatoes together encourages this pest to appear and get a full meal.

Potatoes are prone to a fungal disease known as late blight. When this fungus spreads, it rots the potato. Incidentally, this is what caused the Potato Famine of the nineteenth century in Ireland. Tomatoes and other members of the nightshade family are also susceptible to blight, so don't plant them together, and don't plant tomatoes anywhere there is a history of potato blight because the disease can overwinter and destroy crops the next year.

Other **nightshade** and **brassica** family members such as cabbage, cauliflower, brussels sprouts, kohlrabi, and broccoli can and will inhibit the growth of your tomatoes.

Finally, **black walnut trees** can have a negative effect on many plants, but especially those in the nightshade family.

and one that we strongly encourage, to pinch off all but the uppermost leaves of a mature seedling before replanting. Then when you do replant, bury all but the top third of the plant itself. What was once the plant's stem will now become part of the root system, resulting in increased stability, strength, and growth potential.

Hardening Tomatoes

The next big step in successfully growing tomatoes is the hardening process. In a nutshell, hardening refers to getting your tomato seedlings acclimated to the outdoors. While they have been inside, they have been virtually incubated with temperatures in the 70s (21˚C–26˚C), but the hardening process can begin as soon as the temperatures outside are staying around 55˚F (13˚C). To begin the hardening process, take your seedlings outdoors on a calm, sunny day for a few hours at a time, bringing them back indoors at night for a few days. After a week (assuming the temperature and current forecast are agreeable), leave the plants outdoors overnight. If you are going to plant your tomatoes in the ground, you can do so at this point. Remember to snip off the leaves leaving only those leaves on the top third of the plant. Bury the plant with only the top third above ground.

Companion Planting With Tomatoes

From TomatoCasual.com.
Companion planting is the art of placing certain plants next to others for mutual benefit—a symbiotic relationship, if you will. Let's take a look at beneficial companion planting for tomatoes.

Borage is an annual, edible herb with lovely blue star-shaped flowers. The leaves are delicious and can be used in salads for a unique addition that will surely get people talking around the dinner table. Borage improves tomato plant health and even makes them taste better. Borage also repels the tomato hornworm, the bane of many a tomato grower.

Young dill also improves the health and growth of tomato plants, though it is important to note that if you do grow dill with tomatoes, you should remove it before it becomes mature because it can have a negative effect on the tomato plants in adulthood and actually stunt tomato growth.

Basil is not just great in tomato sauce, it is also known to ward off spider mites, aphids, and whiteflies, all of which can be a problem with tomatoes in different areas of the country. Basil also attracts bees, so you will realize an increase in tomato pollination when basil is present.

Members of the **Umbelliferae** family are a welcome addition to the tomatoes in your urban garden. Parsnip, carrots, Queen Anne's lace, and parsley all attract hover-flies, which are known to go after many tomato pests.

Are aphids and green shield beetles a problem in your area? Try planting **nasturtiums** with your tomatoes. These beautiful flowers are edible and add a slightly peppery undertone to a salad and can also benefit your tomato plants by warding off fungal diseases.

Likely the most common pairing is tomatoes and **French marigolds** which repel nematodes and whiteflies.

Other plants that can benefit your tomato plants include: lavender, garlic, asparagus, thyme, foxglove, and lemon balm.

Growing Climbing Plants

There is nothing quite as pretty as a living wall of greenery, and the urban gardener has quite a selection of plants to choose from if this is the goal. From beans and peas to cucumbers and cantaloupe, there's a climbing veggie plant to suit your personal taste. What you grow depends entirely on you, just as how you grow it depends on the look you want to achieve. *The look? What the heck are we talking about?*

The look that we are referring to, since you asked, is achieved by deciding what type of mechanism you want to allow your plants to climb. While a simple section of chain-link fence may serve the purpose for the no-nonsense urban gardener to grow pole beans on, others might opt for a more-decorative approach and seek out an antique wrought iron gate upon which to train their English peas.

A basic wood trellis is inexpensive, easy to install, and can be painted or stained to match nearly any outdoor décor. Such a trellis can often be affixed to the wall itself,

(Above) Photo by Jennifer Anne Hohman.

VEGETABLE CHART

Plant	Sunlight Needs	Spacing	Plant Size	Type	Container
Beans (pole)	full sun	12" (30cm)	varies (vine)	annual	yes
Broccoli	full sun	12" (30cm)	8"–12" (20cm–30cm)	annual	yes
Cabbage	full to partial sun	12" (30cm)	36" (91cm) (total size)	annual	yes
Carrots	full to partial sun	2" (5cm)	6"–8" (15cm–20cm)	annual	yes
Cucumber	full sun	36"–48" (91cm–122cm)	varies (vine)	annual	yes
Eggplant	full sun	12"–24" (30cm–61cm)	varies	annual	yes
Lettuce	partial sun	8"–12" (20cm–30cm)	varies	annual	yes
Okra	full sun	18"–24" (46cm–61cm)	48" (122cm)	annual	
Onions (spring)	full sun	not needed	½" (1cm) diameter	biennial	yes
Peppers	full sun	18"–24" (46cm–61cm)	24"–36" (61cm–91cm)	annual	yes
Radishes	full sun	1" (3cm)		annual	yes
Tomatoes	full sun	24" (61cm), vine	48"–60"+ (122cm–152cm+)	annual	yes
Tomatoes	full sun	48" (122cm), bush	varies	annual	yes

creating a living mural, whether your climbing plants are in the ground or in decorative containers below.

An A-frame setup (think about the swing set you had as a kid) works well for climbing and vining plants, such as cucumbers, squash, beans, and peas, and by using a roll of heavy-duty twine, you can turn that simple A-frame into a secret hideaway for your kids.

The Native Plant Urban Garden

From UrbanGardenCasual.com.

Nature is not something that happens only in the vast expanse of the countryside. Even the most urban of cities are home to birds, mammals, bugs, and other wildlife, and those critters depend on native wildflowers, grasses, trees, and other plants to provide food and shelter. Native plants also tend to be deep-rooted and work well to control erosion and improve soil quality.

In the urban landscape, you can find native plants in parks, gardens, or abandoned lots, but these plants are under constant threat from development or invasive species. If you want to bring a little wilderness to your city, you can work to save and grow native plants.

First, educate yourself about what plants are native to your area. Just because you see a flower growing in the wild doesn't mean that it's native. Oxeye daisies, for example, are common across North America but actually native to Europe. On this side of the pond, they crowd out native flowers and don't offer as much wildlife benefit as natives like lupine or milkweed. A good field guide (we like *Newcomb's Wildflower Guide*) should help you sort out which plants are native and which are introduced.

(Right) Photo by Reggie Solomon.

Create a Terrarium With Your Kids

by Chris McLaughlin

What you will need:

- 1 or 2 tiny plants
- 1 2-liter soda bottle with cap
- Scissors
- Small stones or pebbles to allow extra water to flow to the bottom and not waterlog the plants
- Houseplant soil
- Sphagnum moss or Spanish moss—this will act as a screen so the soil won't settle into the rocks as the water flows through. It's also pretty as a finishing touch on top of the soil.
- Activated charcoal—acts as a filter that purifies the water as it cycles up and down the terrarium. Pet stores have this charcoal.

(Left) Photo by Ric Deliantoni.

How to build the terrarium:

1. A parent needs to cut the bottom off of the soda bottle about one-third of the way up. Set the top aside.
2. Put a handful of stones at the bottom of the bottle (1"–2" deep [3cm–5cm]).
3. Sprinkle some charcoal over the pebbles.
4. Place some moss over the charcoal.
5. Add the soil to the layers.
6. Add your plants.
7. Add some moss over the soil and between the plants.
8. Put the soda bottle/terrarium lid over the top, squeezing the bottom so the sides are tucked into the top piece. If you want, cut a little slit on the edge of the bottom piece to help the lid go on.

Chris McLaughlin is the author of *The Complete Idiot's Guide to Composting* and *The Complete Idiot's Guide to Growing Heirloom Vegetables.* Find her on the web at www.asuburbanfarmer.com.

Next, consider growing some native plants in your yard or urban garden plot. Even if you only have a postage stamp-sized lot, you can still turn your front yard into a miniature prairie, woodland, or rain garden, depending on your environment. It will be beautiful and will help to ensure that native species have a home well into the future.

A national native plant organization known as Wild Ones (www.for-wild.org) is a great resource for selecting the right plants for your area, not to mention their tips on how to deal with fussbudget neighbors who think wildflowers look messy or unkempt. You may need to plant native plants into a formal garden design or incorporate elements like a bench, birdbath, or walkway to give your yard a more formal look.

If you want to be a real native-plant champion, you can organize a plant rescue for parcels of land that are slated for development or volunteer to remove invasive plants like European buckthorn or Japanese knotweed from public areas, such as parks or school yards. For plant rescues, make sure that you have someplace to transplant what you dig up, and try to conduct the dig on an overcast day to reduce stress on the plants.

If you're going to be pulling weeds, it's a good idea to have some seeds or plugs to plant in their place. And of course, you should always get permission from the land owner or local authorities before doing work on property that is not your own.

Keep It Growing— Garden Maintenance

It isn't enough to get your garden plants started. You'll have to do a little maintenance to keep those plants happy and productive, but once they begin to produce and you are able to taste the fruits of your labors (pun intended) you will be a gardening convert forever. Despite what you may have heard, garden maintenance isn't really all that difficult if you did a proper job getting your garden started in the first place. You read chapter 4, right? Good. You're doing just fine.

Watering

It would be so nice if plants would just adhere to our schedules and come with the ability to be watered

(Right) Photo by Ric Deliantoni.

101

a set amount on a set schedule. Unfortunately, that's just not the way Mother Nature designed things, so we have to be a little more observant than that. Although every plant's specific water needs are a little different from the next, the majority of garden plants will thrive if the soil is kept moist. When you prepared your container or your garden soil for planting, you ensured adequate aeration and drainage, so you should not have to worry about your plant's roots sitting in excess water. However, overwatering can still cause problems with the root system.

When you're first starting out, the best rule of thumb is to read and heed the advice that is on the seed package or the planter card that came with your seedlings. If your plant didn't come with these instructions, ask an expert at your local garden center or nursery for watering advice and follow it carefully. A good rule of thumb is to remember that you don't judge the soil's moisture on the top layer. Stick your finger down about 1" (3cm) into the earth; if it is dry, then the plant probably needs water.

There are all sorts of methods for watering the urban garden, and they all have their own benefits. But the most effective method for new gardeners is the one that keeps you in touch with your plants. We recommend watering by hand because it allows you to place the exact amount of water you need right where it needs to go.

Whether you use a fancy sprinkling can or a lemonade pitcher, the choice is yours. Just remember that for most plants, watering at soil level is the way to go. Try to avoid splashing soil back up on the plant because this can cause disease and fungi to spread.

One final word about watering is about the water that you use. Some people oppose the use of city water on edible plants because of the addition of chlorine and other chemicals added during the water treatment process. You can reduce the amount of chlorine in this water by filling your buckets or watering containers and allowing them to sit undisturbed for several hours before using, allowing the chlorine to evaporate. If you have access to a rain barrel or other rainwater reclamation method, we definitely recommend using that free water!

Weeding

If there is one thing that gets a bad rep in the gardening world, it has to be weeding. Of course, weeding can be tedious and bothersome, but only if you didn't do a thorough job preparing your garden beds beforehand. You *did* read chapter 4, right? In all seriousness, weeds are going to be a part of gardening no matter what you do, but you've got to respect a plant that is so resilient and resourceful as to be able to persevere, stay alive, and even thrive when the odds are stacked against it. If only our garden plants were so prolific!

This is the point where we tell you that the urban casual gardeners don't use harsh chemical weed killers on their gardens, no matter how annoyed they may become with weeds. Not only are they dangerous, they simply are not necessary. If you have a pest issue, check out natural, chemical-free solutions in the next chapter.

tip Watering is best done early in the morning or late in the evening when the sun and the heat of the day are less likely to evaporate the water before it absorbs into the soil.

(Above) Photo by Ric Deliantoni.

The best way to tackle weeds is to keep your eyes open. When you see a weed appear, pull it right then, before it can grow, spread, or reproduce. That is the single best way to keep weeds at bay, and it works better than any chemical you could come up with.

Fertilizing and Feeding

Fertilizing and feeding your plants is an individualized process that needs great care. There is no single rule that applies to all plants, so it is important that you understand the care and feeding for your specific plants. Chapter 4 has an overview of what is found in fertilizers, but covering the fertilizing requirements of all types of urban garden plants is beyond the scope of this book. We recommend that you ask a local expert about the feeding needs of your plants. You can't go wrong when you ask advice from people in your area whose business it is to help you grow healthy and productive gardens!

Wrap It Up

When you know how to start your garden plants the right way, you have a distinct advantage. The first time you nurture a seed into a seedling that then becomes a plant and nourishes you and your family, you will experience an indescribable sense of purpose and accomplishment that will ensure your place among the ranks of those of us who are hopelessly addicted to gardening for life. No matter what you are growing, don't be afraid to ask for advice from local experts on the best way to grow a particular plant in your urban garden. Take along your completed Garden Evaluation Worksheet from chapter 8 when you visit the nursery or garden center, and you'll have all the info they'll need right at your fingertips!

6 Gardening in Special Situations

The urban gardener might be faced with all sorts of interesting special situations. Anything from a lack of space to a lack of time would be enough to annoy anyone, but when you add pesky visitors to the mix, you'll be ready to throw in the towel unless you are prepared. In this chapter, we'll get you ready for what may come, and we'll address many of these issues and provide you with simple solutions so you can garden on your own terms. From community gardens to maintaining a garden while on vacation to composting, privacy, and pest control, we've got you covered.

Community Gardens

In cities across the country and around the world, communal garden areas are popping up in some of the most unlikely places as thousands of new gardeners step outside of their townhomes, condos, co-ops, and apartment buildings and into community gardens. These gardens are as diverse as the reasons people have for joining them in the first place, but generally speaking, a community garden is a plot of land on which members of a community come together to garden. Though there are exceptions, most such gardens are divided into plots of similar size, and the plots are then assigned to individual gardeners (or to families) to sow and tend as they choose. Although the majority of community gardens involve growing vegetables, herbs, and fruit, there are also those that exist solely to beautify an area.

Why Community Garden?

A common complaint among would-be urban gardeners is the lack of space for making those gardening dreams

(Above) Photo by Ric Deliantoni.

105

Profiles in Casual: Joe Lamp'l a.k.a. joe gardener

(Left) Photo provided by Joe Lamp'l.

Joe Lamp'l may have one of the most well-known green thumbs in the gardening biz, but every once in a while, he wears a digit of a different color. In a perfect partnership with the Fiskars company, the man known the world over as joe gardener designs and builds amazing community garden spaces in areas that need them the most through the Project Orange Thumb program.

First of all, how did you get started gardening?

I think I was born with a green thumb. I just didn't realize it until about age eight. At that time, I accidently broke a branch off of one of my parent's favorite shrubs. Not wanting to get caught, I stuck the branch back in the ground. About a month later, I checked on the branch to see how it was doing. I gave it a gentle tug and it resisted. Wow! This branch had rooted, and I was hooked on horticulture. I haven't stopped since.

Tell us a little about how you came to be involved in Project Orange Thumb?

My love of gardening eventually provided an opportunity to host a national television show on DIY Network. As my public visibility increased, I was able to form some valuable relationships with people and companies that were also involved in gardening and outdoor living. Fiskars was one of those companies. A few years ago, Fiskars signed me as its national spokesperson. Agreeing to be Fiskars' spokesperson was an easy decision for me because I think it is a great company that offers awesome tools. Fiskars also does a lot to inspire gardening and gives back to communities; Project Orange Thumb is a perfect example of that.

How are the sites selected?

Fiskars identifies cities they would like to go into and provide the financial and human resources to create a turnkey garden that's substantial enough to remain a viable garden long after the installation takes place. With the help of each city government, neighborhoods that are socially and economically challenged are identified as candidates. This is where Fiskars focuses, as we believe these areas can most dramatically benefit. Then the difficult process of narrowing it down to just one site begins. It's not easy to pick just one site, but we have no choice.

These are major projects with an average budget around $100,000 each. In the end, we always feel like we've made a great decision in selecting the final site, based on the involvement and appreciation we get from the area residents and community. Project Orange Thumb is an exciting project to be involved with, and I'm honored to be the one to design each garden and oversee every installation.

To find more info on Project Orange Thumb, as well as a list of the incredible gardens they have created, visit www.projectorangethumb.com.

(Above) Photo by Kevin C. Matteson.

(Above) Photo by Lisa Parker.

a reality—especially among those who have no outdoor space to speak of. Local community gardens make it possible for people in urban environments to enjoy the benefits and pleasures of having an outdoor garden to tend while also encouraging interaction with their neighbors. Community gardens can easily become an escape from the fast-paced, hectic lifestyle that so many of us get caught up in these days. Nothing compares to the knowledge that you can go home after a long day and get out of your work clothes, grab your iPod, and spend some time tending your garden space while you chat with your neighbors.

Finding a Community Garden

The best resources for finding a community garden in your area are friends and neighbors. They are the most likely to have had experiences with the local gardens, and because they know you, they are uniquely qualified to give you advice on whether the style of a particular garden is for you. That's right, even a community garden can have a personality, and not all gardens work for all people. Plus, it sometimes helps to know someone, especially if you are in an area (such as Seattle, Washington) with such a particularly vibrant community of urban gardeners that there are waiting lists for community garden plots.

Community Gardens:

- Encourage self-reliance

- Save people money on food

- Foster involvement and inter-action with your neighbors

- Provide support for food banks that feed the hungry

- Beautify and enrich the sur-rounding area

Types of Community Gardens

There are several different types of community gardens, and the ones in your area may be governed differently than those in another neighbor-hood. Each garden is set up and run based on the needs and desires of the community it is in, thus the name—community garden. Although many such gardens are run based on organic principles, some exist solely to beautify an area, and as such, the tenders don't feel it necessary to be strict on these guidelines.

Most community gardens are plot-based. This means that the garden is divided into individual plots that are then leased to individuals or families who then choose what they grow and are responsible for tending to their plants. There are other gardens that are more communal in nature, mean-ing that the community works together to plant, water, and maintain the garden as a whole, and the gardeners usually donate the produce to a local food bank or similar organization.

Don't know anyone to ask? Fear not, we've got you covered. All you need to do is head over to the American Community Gardening Associa-tion (ACGA) website at www.communitygarden.org and punch in your zip code for a list of gardens in your area. The ACGA database is constantly growing too, so don't get discouraged if you don't see a lot of options the first time you visit.

Starting a Community Garden

Less than a month after I (that's Michael) moved to a neighborhood in northwest Atlanta in 2009, I founded the Riverside Community Garden. Four weeks later, after meeting several families who shared my love for gar-dening and fresh produce, we broke ground with fifteen plots and no run-ning water. While that wasn't my first experience working in a community garden, it was my first time starting one, and it exists to this day as proof that, with determination and drive, anyone can start a community garden.

With careful planning right out of the gate, a new community garden is much more likely to avoid some of the most common bumps in the road. The first step in starting a community garden is to talk to people and

(Above) Photo by Ric Deliantoni.

gauge interest in doing it in the first place. You'll want a core group of interested folks to help you get through the planning process, which can be a little daunting on your own. Here are a few questions to think about during the planning process:

1. Will the garden be organic?
2. Will the garden consist of raised beds, in-ground plots, or a combination of both?
3. Will your community garden be a communal type, where volunteers work collectively, or an individual type, where people lease plots to do their own thing?
4. Is there potential public land available for your garden, or do you have a place in mind?
5. How will you raise any funds necessary for start-up, supplies, and maintenance costs?
6. Is there a water source available, and who will be responsible for it?

If you have trouble locating potential garden property, you might consider asking around in your neighborhood

Guerrilla Gardening

From UrbanGardenCasual.com.

A new style of stealth gardening is secretly being practiced throughout the country, and the trend is growing right under your nose, though you probably had no idea.

Nicknamed "guerrilla gardening," it is the practice of stealth planting to beautify a community. Planting in places that don't belong to you is illegal in many areas (so be careful if you decide to participate, and research the local ordinances first), but that doesn't stop some folks from trying to make the world a better place through plants.

The popular website Treehugger.com suggests these three rules to remember:

1. Use only land that is unused or unwanted.
2. Leave the land in better condition than it was when you found it.
3. Use plants that are hardy, low maintenance, and have a high success rate if you want anyone to sit up and take notice.

If you'd like to read up on guerrilla gardening from firsthand accounts, check out GuerrillaGardening.org. As the website says, "*This blog began as a record of my illicit cultivation around London. It is now a growing arsenal for anyone interested in the war against the neglect of public space and has become a meeting place for guerrilla gardeners around the world.*"

The pages are filled with wonderful pictures of their exploits. There is also a book, *On Guerrilla Gardening: A Handbook for Gardening Without Boundaries* by Richard Reynolds.

for property owners who wouldn't mind allowing part or all of a piece of property to be used as a garden for a specified amount of time. Before making a firm decision on a property for your community garden, check local zoning laws to ensure that you won't be breaking the rules. This won't be an issue in most situations, but it is always best to err on the side of caution.

Whether you are already involved in a local community garden, just getting started or are considering the daunting task of starting one yourself, the most important thing to remember is that a community garden without community is just a garden. Make the most of the experience by using the opportunity to invest time in your neighborhood and getting to know the people you probably rush by on a daily basis on your way to and from work. You can never have too many friends, and finding

friends who share the common bond of gardening is a special thing indeed.

While You Are Away

One of the reasons people in an urban environment give for avoiding gardening is that they don't want to feel tethered to their homes. People who live in the city often enjoy their small quarters because such a lifestyle allows them to travel on the weekends and over holidays. What happens if you start an urban garden—even an indoor one—and want to go away for a few days?

Self-Watering Containers

We talked about self-watering containers in chapter 3, and when it comes to freeing up your time, there's really nothing better than a reliable self-watering system. Most major retailers offer self-watering containers these days, so they are readily accessible nearly anywhere in the country. For those of you who want the convenience of a self-watering device without the expense, we do have an extremely low-cost option for you. If you have a couple of common items around the house, you can create a self-watering device for your planters that will not cost you a single cent.

You Need:

- One 20-ounce plastic bottle
- Hammer
- Small nail
- A sharp knife or razor blade
- Old panty hose

How To Do It:

1. Using the hammer and nail, make several holes in the bottle cap.
2. Using a knife, remove the bottom from the bottle.
3. Cut a small square from the panty hose and place it over the top of the bottle before screwing on the cap. This ensures that nothing will clog the holes.
4. Loosen the soil in a small area to the side of your plant and bury the cap end plus about 1" (3cm) of the bottle itself in the soil close to the plant base.

tip Dedicated DIYers can check chapter 8 for links to self-watering container designs that you can make at home.

5. Fill your self-watering bottle with water and enjoy being stress-free for a few days as your plant is watered automatically.

It is a good idea to pay attention the first couple of times you fill your self-watering device. Knowing how long it takes before your bottle needs to be refilled will tell you how many days you can be away from your plants before they will start getting thirsty again.

Go for a Swim

The biggest problem your plants are going to have while you are away is that they may not have ready access to the water they need. One quick, easy, and inexpensive work-around is to place your plants in the bathtub or sink. Run just an inch or two (about three centimeters) of water in the basin, and your plants can soak it up as they need it. This may not be the ideal option, but it definitely works in a pinch.

Create a Temporary Terrarium

If your plants are indoors or you can move them to an outdoor area that is less exposed to direct sunlight and the elements, another option is to create a makeshift terrarium. Don't stress—it is actually simple to do and probably will not cost a thing.

Water your plants well by placing their container in a larger container and filling that container with an inch or so (about 3cm) of water and refilling the larger container until the plant will no longer soak up more liquid. Next, take a large clear plastic bag (such as the kind that covers your clothes when you pick them up at the dry cleaner) and place your plant inside the bag. Fill it with air and secure the openings so the air remains inside.

(Left) Photo by Gia Marie Houck.

Your temporary terrarium will allow moisture to accumulate at the top of the bag and then "rain" back down onto the plant with a minimum of moisture loss. This can often buy you several days away from home with minimal impact on your greenery.

Friends and Neighbors

One of the most convenient ways to ensure that your plants are being looked after while you are away from home is to ask a friend or neighbor to check on them. Most people have someone bringing in their mail during an extended absence, so it isn't that big of a stretch to ask a friend or neighbor to water the plants as well.

If this is the option you choose, keep in mind that not everyone knows the ins and outs of watering plants—when, how, or how much—and as such, it may be a good idea to leave your volunteer water brigade with some instructions to guide them. It shouldn't take more than a few words to detail your plant's hydration needs, and the extra information might mean the difference between returning home to find lush, thriving greenery or plants that have been over- or under-watered to death.

Hire a Plant Pro

Believe it or not, there are people who make a living taking care of plants. Although this career hasn't really caught on as the next big thing, there are plant-sitters in major cities across the country now. If you are having trouble locating one in your area check with businesses that have live greenery indoors. Plant pros generally advertise to these businesses because the businesses typically do not want the responsibility of maintaining the plants, replacing them, or updating them at different times of the year.

Cans and Cant's of Composting

You *can* compost vegetables and fruit that hasn't been cooked, but you *can't* compost the leftover stew in your fridge.

You *can* compost coffee grounds, tea leaves, and tea bags, but you *can't* compost coffee or tea with sugar or cream.

(Above) Photos by Reggie Solomon.

Regardless of what form your urban gardening efforts take, it is still entirely possible to take a few days off for a well-deserved vacation now and then, and with a bit of careful preparation and forethought on your part, your plants will never even know you are gone. Whether you have a friend or neighbor play babysitter, use an irrigation system or hire a professional, you can rest easy knowing that you will return from your trip relaxed and rejuvenated to find your garden greener and more lush than ever.

Composting in the Urban Garden

Across America, our landfills are being filled at an alarming rate. Simply put, we are running out of space to dump our trash! Although it may sound hopeless on the surface, there is good news according to the Environmental Protection Agency, which tells us that the two biggest space hogs in landfills in the United States are food and paper. Why is this good news? Because neither food waste nor paper need to go to the landfills. They can be recycled.

To give you a better idea of just how much food and paper are literally being thrown away, these two categories account for more than half of all landfill waste—that's more than diapers, plastics, tires, and Styrofoam combined! When you take into account how much the average person tosses into the landfill every week, recycling your food and paper waste into compost just makes sense.

When you compost, you not only help the environment by not adding as much to the landfill, you also create some of the most nutrient-rich planting material available—and it's free. If you live in an urban environment, chances are you have probably never given composting much thought, but the truth is that you can compost successfully even in the city.

(Above) Photo by Matt Montagne.

(Above) Photo by Joel Ignacio.

Composting is so easy that it will happen even if you don't do anything.

What to Compost

Let's take a look at the tremendous variety of items that can successfully be composted. Although it is true that food can generally be composted, there are a few rules about what types of food should go into your compost pile and some definite items to steer clear of. A good rule of thumb is to remember that with very few exceptions, anything that is plant-based should be composted, while anything that is animal-based should not.

Even people who are composting veterans often miss out on some things that can go into the compost bin. Here are a few interesting items that you should add to your composting list:

- Office paper
- Fireplace ash
- Eggshells
- Dryer lint
- Tea bags
- Coffee grounds and filters
- Shredded newspaper
- Shredded cotton rags
- Shredded wool rags
- Houseplant trimmings
- Hair and fur
- Fingernail clippings
- Paper towel rolls
- Dead cut-flower arrangements
- Seafood shells

What Not to Compost

One rookie mistake when it comes to composting relates to those things that should not be composted. It's easy to get into the habit that all food goes to the composter, but the problem is that not all food items are compostable. Animal products, including meat, skin, bones, and fat, should not be composted. Likewise for milk and other dairy products. Animal-based products can often contain harmful bacteria and even the potential for disease that can spread throughout the compost pile.

How to Compost in an Urban Environment

Perhaps you have skimmed this section thus far because you didn't think it really applied to you. Urban gardeners have long been forgiven for not composting because of a lack of proper outdoor space that was conducive to such practices. Let's face it, you just don't have anywhere to put a compost bin.

There are two options for you, and both are easy to do. Most community gardens have a community compost on site. This first option provides a place for urban garden folk to take their compostable waste, and in turn, it becomes a nutrient-rich soil amendments that will help the community garden grow bigger and more-productive plants in the future. You can easily take advantage of the community site by placing your compost material in a designated container that you regularly take to the site to empty.

We've talked to thousands of people just like you in cities across the country, and in recent years, an increasing number of them are getting worms! No, we don't mean they're falling victim to something you're likely to see on the next prime-time medical drama. The second composting option for urban gardeners with limited space

is known as *vermiculture* or vermicomposting, and it is becoming more and more popular, even among folks who never thought for a second they would be raising worms.

How Does Vermicomposting Work?

Vermicomposting is the process of using worms to speed up the decomposition of compostable waste products into a usable, beneficial soil amendment that is most commonly referred to in polite circles as *worm casings*. Those of us who are slightly less inclined to be proper understand and accept that we're talking about worm poop.

Now before you go getting grossed out, you should know that worm casings are incredibly good for the soil, and you will pay a premium price for this soil amendment at high-end garden centers around the country. With a little preparation, you can produce your own worm casings time and time again, and you just might find that those worms aren't as disgusting as you first thought.

The basic vermicomposting setup includes three primary components

- A good-sized sturdy container with a lid
- A supply of shredded newspaper for dry bedding (black and white pages only—no glossy pages)
- A pound of vermicomposting worms

The container can be a simple plastic storage bin with a secure-fitting lid. You will need to drill a series of small holes in the container and lid for adequate air flow, but don't worry, as long as their food source is inside the container that is where the worms are going to stay. One small hole every 2" (5cm) or so should be adequate. Into the container first goes a good amount of shredded newspaper bedding. Next come the worms.

On first glance, *Eisenia foetida* or *Lumbricus rubellaus* might seem like something you need antibiotics for, but they are two breeds of worms that are used in vermicomposting. You can't use just any type of worm for this process, and not all worms are created equal, so be sure to look for names like brandlings, manure worms, red worms, red wrigglers, or tiger worms to know you're getting the right type. One final note on worm types: Some unscrupulous vendors may have you believe that their worms are some sort of special, high-performance hybrid breed that will outperform the competition. Don't buy it; there is no such thing as a hybrid worm, period.

You can start your vermicomposting container with 1 pound (½kg) of worms added right on top of the shredded newspaper. Cover the bin and give them about 15 minutes to start getting settled into their new home before you feed them. Incidentally, you can feed your worms the same things you can put into a regular compost bin. Here are a few guidelines to keep in mind:

- It is good to chop compostable materials into small pieces because they will be more easily consumed.
- Watch how moist you let things get. Worms can (and will) drown if you allow your bin to get soupy.
- Don't let your bin get too hot or too cold, or you will end up with a bin full of dead worms and rotting vegetable matter. A temperature range of between 60°F and 75°F (16°C and 24°C) will be ideal.
- If you overfill your container, it will begin to smell. This is a sure sign that your worms are unable to eat the amount of food that you are giving them. Back off on adding additional food for a few days until the smell dissipates and the available food has been consumed.

Types of Vermicomposting

Now that you know the basics of how worm-poop farming works (sorry, we couldn't resist), let's take a look at the three distinct types of vermicomposting:

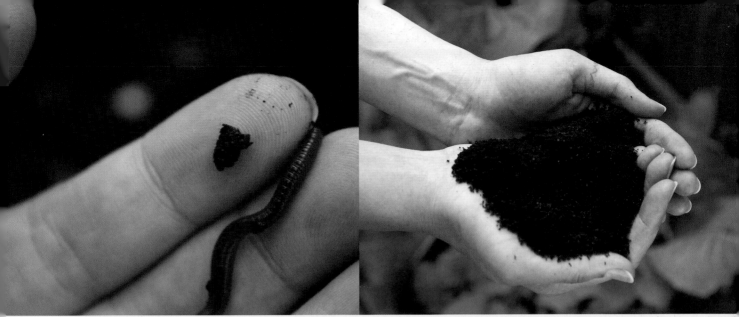

(Above) Photo by Ric Deliantoni.

Noncontinuous vermicomposting is the most basic, and generally most labor intensive, form of worm farming. The description mentioned above is an example of the noncontinuous method. Although it doesn't require all that much effort on a day-to-day basis, when it comes time to harvest your worm casings you will see what I mean. The entire contents of your bin must be dumped and sorted by hand, and you must start fresh, thus the name. The casings will usually need to be harvested every three months or so, and you will know when it is time when all of the food and bedding has been digested and is no longer recognizable.

Continuous vertical vermicomposting is one alternative that might appeal to you. Using a series of stacked trays, one on top of the next, you fill the trays, starting with the bottom tray first. The first layer is not harvested, instead being covered with a second tray onto which the organic material is then placed. When the worms are finished with the bottom tray they will migrate upward, leaving the lower tray to be harvested with just a few stragglers that can be added to the upper trays by hand.

Continuous horizontal vermicomposting operates on the same principle as its vertical cousin, but as the name might imply, it works side by side instead of vertically. A long tray is divided into two sections that are separated by a large-gauge chicken wire wall. Bedding, worms, and organic matter are added to one side at a time. When it is time to harvest, fresh bedding and food is added to the empty side. Over time, the worms will migrate, allowing you to harvest your casings and begin the process anew.

Construct your own composter, start a vermicomposter, or take your organic refuse to a community compost pile. No matter which option you choose, you are making an impact on the world around you by reducing the amount of waste that ends up in our landfills. You are also improving the quality of the soil that will in turn nourish you. All in all, you have to admit that composting is a win-win situation all the way around.

(Left) Photo by Korina Adkins.

Urban Garden Style

Regardless of the form your urban garden takes or where it is located, chances are good that you are going to want to infuse it with your personal style. No matter how large or small your space is, there are all sorts of ways to make that happen. One of the easiest ways to get an eye-catching look is to incorporate plant size, color, and shape into your overall design concept to create a custom-tailored look in any garden space. Check chapter 8 for some can't-miss resources that will help.

Dress It Up!

You might think that city gardens are all boring terra cotta pots and a whole lot of same old, same old, but you couldn't be more wrong. You've got style, and everybody knows it. Don't be afraid to infuse your urban garden space with a little of that good taste as well. In fact, some of the very same ideas that you use for decorating your home can be used in the urban garden space as well.

Flower Pot or Art? We're not going to imply even for a moment that plain terra cotta pots don't have their place in the world, but chances are that place isn't in your garden, right? You take time to make sure that every detail of your home is just the way you like it, and you shouldn't have to settle for less than that in your garden. With an hour and some specially formulated paint—available at any craft store—you can create a one-of-a-kind masterpiece that will be the envy of the neighborhood.

Paint too tame for your tastes? A bit of mortar and a few broken tiles, bits of glass, and even broken china can transform those plain pots into amazing works of art that you will be proud to show off at every opportunity.

Contain It

What if all you need is a way to contain your containers, to tie them all together in some sort of cohesive appearance that belongs on the society pages? That's when you really need to start thinking outside—or inside—the box. Literally. Wine crates, decorative boxes, even discarded dresser drawers can become quick, quirky, and functional containers for your little garden gems.

The only limits here are the ones you place on yourself. Well, okay, so there are a few other limits (including good taste), but as long as you aren't going to stuff a tomato plant into an old toilet on your front stoop, you should be in good shape. Don't let your preconceived notions about how gardens are *supposed* to look get in your way. You have the power and the flexibility to make your urban garden space as personal and individual as your home is, and with a little imagination and effort, you will do just that. For more ideas about making the most of your urban garden style, visit UrbanGardenCasual.com.

Natural Privacy in Your Garden

From UrbanGardenCasual.com.

One of the most annoying things about gardening in the city can be how much attention it draws. Because most urban dwellers can't build anything permanent at most rental locations, use your creativity to fashion temporary climbing walls and place them in an arrangement that affords you privacy where you need it most. Grow plants that vine easily: cucumbers, green beans, squash, etc.

A favorite low-cost tool for use in urban gardens is none other than the simple wooden pallet. You can even paint them to look better while your plants get their start.

You can also use scrap lumber or even old gates and fencing to give your plants a great place to climb.

Another great temporary privacy solution for your urban garden is sunflowers. They grow uberfast and will make all the neighbors jealous at the same time. Not to mention that you can save the seeds for delicious snacks and additions to salads.

Although it is possible to use a natural privacy screen in a variety of places, we don't recommend you use them in areas such as fire escapes or other emergency access areas that may be impeded by its inclusion. Keep these areas clear and free from obstacles. Use discretion and caution when making a decision about where to include your privacy plantings.

Building a Water Garden and Wildlife Pond

From UrbanGardenCasual.com.

Water features are popular with many homeowners. A pond makes an attractive addition to your garden, and creating one to attract wildlife requires much less maintenance than the traditional fish pond. By following a few simple rules, you will attract wildlife and transform your urban garden into a serene oasis of beauty.

Getting Started

A wildlife pond should never be more than 3' (1m) deep. This is deep enough to allow frogs to thrive but is still a safe depth for the home garden. Planting the pond with various species of native plants will ensure that your pond attracts a variety of wildlife.

Digging

When building a pond, a fiberglass preformed liner can be used, but it is far less expensive and will look more natural to dig a pond and line it yourself with rubber pond liner available at most landscaping supply stores. When digging your own shape, bear in mind that ovals are most like natural ponds. Add in various places to plant by digging a series of steps into the side of your pond.

After digging out the hole, check to make sure each step and the bottom of the pond is perfectly level. Ignoring this step will be very noticeable after the pond is filled with water and much harder to correct later on. Leveling the pond is probably the only difficult step in building a small pond, and it is very important from an aesthetic standpoint.

Make A Simple DIY Holiday Tree

A plain-Jane wire tomato cage can easily and quickly become an ingenious holiday garden decoration. If you are repurposing a cage you used previously, be sure to clean it well before you get started (a little sandpaper can help to clean up those wayward rust spots).

Step 1: Start by bending the anchor stakes (the ends that go into the ground) toward the center to form a point. Sometimes these cages have a mind all their own, so if you find it necessary, use a twist tie to keep the ends together. This will be the top of your tree.

Step 2: Beginning at the point and working toward the bottom, wrap the cage with inexpensive tinsel, securing with twist ties as needed.

Step 3: Wrap a strand of holiday lights from top to bottom, being sure to start with the end that does not need to be plugged in.

That's all there is to it! You now have a quick, inexpensive, and unique urban garden decoration that you won't have to stow away after the holidays. If you are going to use this outdoors, be sure to use lights that are rated for indoor and outdoor use, and secure your holiday tree by tying it to something sturdy. You don't want a random gust of wind to blow your decoration to the North Pole!

(Above) Photo by Ric Deliantoni.

Lining the Pond

To calculate the amount of rubber pond liner you'll need, first double the depth. Take that figure and add it to the length. Then add in a 1' (30cm) overlap. Then take the doubled depth and add it to the width and add in a 1' (30cm) overlap. For example, a pond that is 3' (1m) deep, 4' (1.2m) wide and 6' (1.8m) long will need a liner that is 11' (3.4m) wide and 13' (4m) long. You will also need an underlay cut to the same dimensions as your liner.

After checking one last time to make sure the pond is level, place the underlay into the hole, adjusting and straightening it as much as possible. It will look wrinkled, but it doesn't matter because it eventually will be covered in water. Next lay the rubber liner. This is definitely a two-person job, so save yourself the embarrassment of being seen falling backward into a hole because you didn't ask for help.

Make sure the liner lays loosely in the hole and that it overlaps the hole all the way around the edge. Next line the edge of your pond with rocks. This will hold the liner in place and will hide it as well. The rocks will also give frogs and insects a place to sit near the water. When working with stones, make sure to lay them firmly against each other so there is very little wiggle. This will ensure that your pond is safe for children and pets. When your liner is laid and the rocks are in place, fill the pond with water.

Planting the Pond

Now that you've seen how wonderful your wildlife pond looks filled with water, the next step is to choose a variety of aquatic plants that are native to your area. Most ponds are small, but don't let that discourage you. We know of home water gardens that have as many as twenty species of native plants in or near them! Those plant species can attract an awe-inspiring variety of birds, butterflies, dragonflies, frogs, toads, and more. To plant the pond, leave the plants in their pots and arrange the pots in the water.

Pest Control in the Urban Garden

The Urban Garden Casual philosophy dictates that we try to keep things natural and organic whenever possible, but when it comes to pest control in the urban garden, there are times when even we are tempted to reach for the napalm and let the leaves fall where they may. Okay, so that's only a partial exaggeration, but suffice it to say that based on the number of e-mails and website comments

Build a Japanese Beetle Trap

Although mechanical traps are available commercially for successfully capturing Japanese beetles, you may want to give this homemade version a try.

You will need:

- ½ cup water
- ⅛ cup sugar
- ½ banana
- 1 package of yeast
- Empty milk or orange juice carton

1. Place all the ingredients in a blender and blend them until well mixed and the banana is pureed.

2. Pour the mixture into a milk or orange juice carton and hang or set it in the infestation area with the lid left off.

The Japanese beetles will be attracted to the scent and will fly into the carton to investigate. They will not be able to fly back out of the carton.

Make Your Own Garden Pest Spray

You will need:

- 25 cloves garlic (or 2 large bulbs)
- 2 tablespoons cayenne pepper or 2 fresh hot peppers
- 2 tablespoons dish detergent
- 1 tablespoon vegetable oil
- 6 cups fresh water

1. Mix the first four ingredients in a blender with 2 cups of water and blend very well, about 2 minutes.

2. Allow the mixture to sit for about an hour undisturbed, and then strain it through a fine-mesh strainer or cheesecloth.

3. Add the remaining 4 cups of water and add the mixture to a spray bottle. Spray the plants and ground surface area, being careful to spray both sides of the leaves and stalks.

4. Repeat daily until the pests are eradicated, and then use as needed.

Store the extra mixture in a jar with a tight-fitting lid and mark it well!

we have received on the topic of pest control, we know we aren't the only ones who are bugged by bugs in the garden.

Insect Control Using Household Products

One of the most effective and least harmful methods for insect control on outdoor plants is using regular *household vinegar*. First, inspect your plant and remove any insects that you find. Next make a 1-to-1 mixture of vinegar and water in a spray bottle and spray the entire plant, including the underside of the leaves.

Another low-cost, low-toxicity option is to make a diluted soap mixture by adding 3–5 tablespoons of a simple, inexpensive dishwashing detergent (not the kind used in dishwashers) to a gallon of water.

Japanese Beetles

The Japanese beetle is easily one of the most feared garden pests in the eastern United States. The adult beetle feeds on leaves and foliage, leaving bare skeletons where the lush foliage used to be, while the immature grubs feed on the roots. They are a problem for many gardeners, both beginner and experienced, and they can do a lot of damage in a short amount of time, but how do you deal with them when they show up?

Treatment With Chemical Agents. Even the most environmentally aware urban gardener may be tempted to go for the chemical insecticides when Japanese beetles appear—they can be just that frustrating to eradicate. Chemical agents, such as acephate and malathion, are used routinely to treat adult beetles, while isofenphos, diazinon, and others are used to treat larval-stage beetles.

Treatment With Biological Agents. Given a bit more patience and some time, long lasting results can be realized through the use of biological agents that are far less damaging to the environment. Such biological approaches might include the use of bacteria, nematodes, and fungi and should be discussed with your local Extension agent or another well-trained professional before proceeding. These professionals have probably already gone through this more than once and will be in a great position to help you get through your Japanese beetle infestation without losing all of your garden and your hair.

Treatment With Resistant Plants. We encourage the use of beetle-resistant plants as a method of discouraging these pests from taking up residence in your garden. Plants such as zinnias (white and pastel colors), wild berries and grapes, soybeans, evening primrose, and African marigolds are not only beautiful, but they are proven to resist infestation, as are white roses. If you make it through one Japanese beetle infestation, you will swear by these beauties!

reader tip "I used to live in California where aphids were always a problem for gardeners. It was there that I learned to light two cigarettes and stick the butt ends in the ground near an aphid-infested plant. Then just cover the plant with a bucket or trash can and leave it in place for an hour, and just like that, the aphids are gone."

Animals and Rodents

When I (Michael) was first asked to write about the issue of cats in the garden, it took me a while to figure out how to approach the topic, but eventually it was obvious that my efforts were appreciated. In May 2008, I wrote this post for UrbanGardenCasual.com and it remains one of the most popular on the site to this day, so reprinted here for your information and enjoyment is that blog post:

Now before I come across as a kitty hater, I should tell you that I have a cat, and I love him dearly.

Chance lives inside. He eats aloe and poops on my kitchen rugs when he wants the litter box to be cleaned. Trust me, if you think cat crap in your petunias is bad, try squishing it between your toes as you reach for your first cup of coffee in the morning. Sometimes I want to love Chance to death.

Here are a few tips to make your personal garden area much less susceptible to feline attacks:

1. When you find kitty gifts (that's cat crap to most of you), you must remove them. Before I caught on to this, the cats in my garden routinely used my containers as their own personal toilets.

2. If you keep the soil damp, cats are less likely to mess with it. They hate water, see? I have had particular fun while using an inexpensive, long-range water pistol purchased at a toy store years ago and never given to the tot for whom it was intended. Did I mention that cats hate water? It's true.

3. Cats also hate blood meal, and it is a great fertilizer.

4. Chicken wire or wire screening around the base of your plants will keep cats at bay, at least in your plants' immediate vicinity.

uses the three things that garden pests loathe the most: water, noise, and the element of surprise. The concept is so simple you will wish that you had come up with it.

Imagine watching over your casual garden from a stealth location when suddenly a pest appears, poised to bring havoc and horror to your carefully cultivated greenery. Immediately you pull out the big guns—the water guns, that is—and liberally soak down the area while making plenty of noise. The pest disappears. Problem solved—until that time when you're not around, right? Well, what if there were an automated water cannon that could handle the watch for you?

The ScareCrow Motion-activated Animal Deterrent (manufactured by Contech Enterprises, Inc.) does exactly that; it keeps an "eye" out for trespassers in your garden, thanks to a built-in, battery-operated motion sensor. Upon critter detection, the ScareCrow immediately shoots a three second burst of water right at the offender while making a quick and sudden sound that is sure to scare off even the most cocksure garden visitor. Not only is the ScareCrow simple to use and effective, it uses no chemicals whatsoever, which means it is suitable and safe for use around pets and children and in any organic garden environment.

No matter who you are or where you live, from the potato farms of Idaho to the rooftop gardens of Brooklyn, you are going to have to battle pests at some point. If you keep a clean urban garden space and take precautions, like covering surfaces with chicken wire, the majority of pests can be easily handled with minimal loss.

For more resources on pest control in your garden, check out chapter 8.

5. Plant a nice patch of catnip well away from your edible plants. The cats will love you for it and may even be nice enough to stop leaving you crappy gifts.

Anything you can do to cover bare soil—especially soil that is freshly dug—will keep them at bay. And by them I mean the cats in your garden, not the plants. You don't want to keep the plants at bay.

The Scarecrow Revisited

It took years to materialize, but we have finally found an animal and rodent deterrent that is fully worthy of Urban Garden Casual's seal of approval. Instead of harsh chemicals or clumsy construction ideas, the ScareCrow sprinkler

Gardening With Kids

From UrbanGardenCasual.com.

Make a commitment this gardening season to get kids out in the garden. Older children can create a gardening budget, plan the layout of the garden, plant, and help maintain the garden—even if it is a container garden. They also can create a cookbook of recipes using the fresh produce your family grows. Younger children can help plant and care for the garden along with learning how to harvest the family's bounty. Here are two crafty ideas to get your family garden started:

Grassheads #1

(ages 2–5 years)
You will need:

- Egg carton
- Eggshells, broken fairly cleanly in half
- Soil
- Grass seed or chives
- Markers

Wash out the eggshells and let them dry. While they are drying, cut apart the cups in the egg carton. Give each child half an eggshell and let them decorate the shells like faces. Orientate the faces so the open side of the shell is the top of the head. After they finish decorating the shells have the children place their creation in one of the eggcups from the carton. They can decorate the carton cup as clothing or the rest of the body.

Fill the eggshell with soil and sprinkle it with grass seed or chives. Gently water your grasshead. Please note that watering your grasshead is something that you will have to do often to keep the plant growing. When the seeds germinate, the child can cut the grasshead's hair to any style and it will grow back again for another trim or new do.

Grassheads #2

(ages 6–100 years)
You will need:

- Panty hose or knee-highs
- Soil
- Grass seed or chives
- Cup
- Decorations

Cut the leg off the panty hose or use knee-highs and fill the foot with seed. Then fill with soil until it forms a round head shape and tie off tightly. Cut off the excess panty hose so that the head sits on top of a cup with the bottom knot and some of the panty hose left inside the cup. This tail of panty hose will act as a wick and help water the grasshead.

Next decorate your grasshead with buttons, ribbon, markers, or anything your kids can come up with to personalize each person's grasshead. Fill your cup with water and place your grasshead in the cup with the panty hose tail tucked inside. This grasshead will self-water using this wicking system. After your seeds germinate, you can style your grasshead's hair to your liking over and over again.

Although these activities may seem minor, they create teaching opportunities where some of the most valuable knowledge is learned. These moments are about more than making a craft or growing a seed, and regardless of where you live, these activities help preserve the agricultural knowledge base that we are losing with each generation.

7 Urban Casual Recipes

Now that you have grown your urban bounty, you will no doubt need a few hot new ideas on how to use those gorgeous fruits and veggies, and we have you covered. In keeping with the Urban Garden Casual philosophy, the recipes you will find in this chapter are chilled out and relaxed—perfect for a quiet evening for two or a get-together with a few friends. The best part is that each of these dishes will spotlight those delectable edibles that you grew yourself in conjunction with other ingredients that are healthy, local, and sustainable.

Casual Drinks

Reggie's Ultimate Urban Mojito

  2 teaspoons powdered sugar

  Juice from 1 lime

  8–10 fresh mint leaves

  1½ oz. rum

  Club soda

  Ice

  Mint, lime wedges, and sugar cane sticks
    for garnish

1. In a tall glass, mix the lime juice, mint, and sugar.
2. In the glass, crush the mint into the sugar with a muddler or the back of a spoon.
3. Add the rum and ice, and fill to the top with club soda, garnishing with mint, lime wedge, and frozen sugar cane stick.

tip Most people might not think about using fresh goodies from their own garden to make drinks, but they are truly missing out. Bartenders in finer establishments have been doing it for years, and now so can you.

Profiles in Casual: The Shibaguyz

Location: Seattle, Washington
USDA Hardiness Zone: 8

Shannon Mullet-Bowlsby lives in the epicenter of the Pacific Northwest—Seattle, Washington. He and his partner, Jason, have made quite a name for themselves in the urban gardening community, both at home on the small patio they lovingly refer to as "The Jungle" and in community gardens around the area.

What is your hardiness zone?

We are in Zone 8. Seattle is located between Puget Sound and the Cascade Mountains in a band very similar to the Mediterranean. We get a lot of rain in the winter months but rarely have temperatures below 40°F (4°C) or above 80°F (27°C). Also, because we are located in the midst of a volcanic range (Mount Rainier, Mount St. Helens, and Mount

Baker are easily seen from the city on clear days), the soil is excellent for growing just about anything.

When did you first become interested in community gardens?

We have been involved with gardens and urban gardening since our childhoods. It was a daily occurrence in our childhoods to be invited over to the neighbors' to pick beans or squash. This is just a continuation of that. Shortly after moving to Seattle twenty years ago, I was made aware that the city was the home of the first recognized P-Patch in the United States.

NOTE: P-Patch is a term that's specific to Seattle, Washington, where the Picardo family allotted part of their farm to be used as the first community garden in the city. Thus the P in the name "P-Patch." Since that time, the patch has grown to include more than seventy-five separate community garden areas throughout the city.

Seattle actively recruits individuals to get involved in community gardening and buys urban property to convert to community gardens. There is currently a waiting list of one year for many of the locations throughout the city.

What do you find to be the most surprising aspect of community gardening?

There are two things I have noticed. Many folks are afraid to take chances unless they have a lot of support or goading. For example, if one gardener has a bad year with his or her tomatoes, suddenly everyone is talking about how you just can't grow good tomatoes in Seattle, and many won't try them again. Rather than asking a local Master Gardener for tips, they just give up. Also, others think that growing food is so much harder than growing flowers. They are all plants with unique needs; but in the end, the process is the same. As far as I'm concerned, if I get a bowlful of chili made from my own beans, onions, and tomatoes, it's worth it every time!

What have been your biggest successes?

We have a great success rate of growing tomatoes in the Northwest. The trick is to find varieties that are meant for your growing season. Because it is relatively cool most of the summer, large tomatoes have a hard time ripening before it gets too cold. Through trial and error, we have found a number of amazing smaller salad tomatoes and some excellent cold-hardy heirlooms that provide bumper crops.

What about failures? Any you would want to share?

Don't laugh. Zucchini. *No, really!* Everyone in the country has more than they can eat, and we maybe get one or two pitiful little pencil-thick squash. I don't know why, and I don't like talking about it.

The other is peppers. The cool climate of Seattle is excellent for most every fruit or veggie, but true heat-loving peppers have a hard time thriving. We let the folks on the other side of the mountains grow them and bring them to us.

Cucumber-Infused Gin

3 cucumbers fresh from the garden

1 bottle of good quality gin

1. Peel, seed, and dice the cucumbers and place them in a large, lidded pitcher.
2. Pour the entire bottle of gin over the cucumbers and cover. Leave to sit undisturbed at room temperature for three days.
3. Strain the cucumbers from the gin using cheese-cloth draped over a mesh strainer. Pour the filtered gin back into the bottle, add a label and enjoy!

This will keep at room temperature for 6 months. No refrigeration is necessary.

Minty-Fresh Lemonade

1½ cups sugar

½ cup boiling water

1 tablespoon freshly grated lemon peel

1½ cups freshly squeezed lemon juice

1 peel from squeezed lemon, not grated

¼ cup packed fresh mint leaves

Lemon slices and mint leaves for garnish

1. Mix the boiling water with the sugar and grated lemon peel.
2. Add the whole lemon peel and mint leaves, and let the mixture stand for 30 minutes.
3. Strain out the whole peel, add the fresh lemon juice and serve over ice, garnished with a lemon slice and mint leaf.

Casual Apps and Sides

Swiss Chard

Along with some good cheese, fresh tomato slices, some pickles, and maybe some sliced salami, this makes a nice appetizer to enjoy with a glass of wine.

> 2 pounds fresh chard, cleaned and roughly chopped
>
> 1 small sweet onion, chopped
>
> 4 cloves garlic
>
> ½ tablespoon of fresh basil (or ½ teaspoon dried)
>
> ½ tablespoon of fresh oregano (or ½ teaspoon dried)
>
> Salt to taste
>
> Freshly ground black pepper to taste
>
> 3 tablespoons olive oil
>
> 3 tablespoons red wine vinegar

1. In a large sauté pan, cook the onion over medium heat in olive oil.
2. When the onion just begins to brown, add the chard and garlic, herbs, salt, and pepper and sauté until the chard is tender.
3. Remove from heat, add the vinegar and allow to cool slightly before serving.

Roasted Vegetables

> 4 new red potatoes, washed, dried, each cut into 8 pieces
>
> 4 new beets, peeled and cut into quarters
>
> 1 sweet onion, cut into quarters and separated
>
> 1 large handful of green beans
>
> 1 medium eggplant, cut into cubes
>
> 3 cloves garlic, minced
>
> 1 teaspoon fresh rosemary
>
> 3 tablespoons olive oil
>
> Salt to taste
>
> Freshly ground black pepper to taste

1. Preheat the oven to 400°F (203°C). Place the olive oil in a large roasting pan and place the pan in the preheated oven for 5 minutes.
2. Carefully remove the pan from the oven. Add all the vegetables to the pan, tossing them in the olive oil.
3. Add the salt, pepper, garlic, and rosemary and mix thoroughly.
4. Bake at 400°F (203°F) until the potatoes are tender, about 40 minutes.

(Below) Photo by Howard Walfish.

Too Hot in the Kitchen Tomato Salad

4 large ripe tomatoes, ideally in different colors

½ cup pitted kalamata olives, halved

¼ pound feta cheese

2 tablespoons fruity olive oil

2 tablespoons red wine vinegar

Fresh ground black pepper to taste

1. Chop the tomatoes into bite-sized pieces.
2. Add the olives and crumble the feta over the top.
3. Whisk the vinegar and olive oil together and drizzle over the salad.
4. Season to taste with pepper, toss gently, and get back outside!

Variations

- Add a peeled, chopped cucumber to the tomato.
- For a more robust taste, add a crushed clove of garlic to the oil and vinegar.
- For a lighter taste, use the juice of one lemon instead of vinegar.
- Chop the tomatoes smaller and use as a bruschetta topping.
- This makes a good pasta sauce, too, but then you have to turn on the stove.

Sometimes all you need is the perfect comple-ment to your entrée, and these amazing appetiz-ers and side dishes deliver all the taste and pizzazz you need to make your urban garden the centerpiece of any meal.

Simple Summer Pickles

3 large cucumbers

1 red bell pepper

1 onion

1 tablespoon sea salt

2 teaspoons celery seed

½ cup white vinegar

¼ cup granulated sugar

1. Wash the cucumbers and slice them about ⅛" (3mm) thick into a medium-sized bowl. *Don't remove the peel!*
2. Wash and deseed the pepper, peel the onion, and finely chop both. Add both to the cucumbers.
3. Sprinkle liberally with sea salt and celery seed, cover and allow to sit undisturbed for an hour.
4. In a saucepan, boil the vinegar and immediately remove it from the heat. Stir in the sugar until it dissolves and allow the mixture to cool.
5. Mix the vegetables and the marinade well, cover and refrigerate no less than 24 hours before serving, preferably at least 3 days.
   Keeps refrigerated for two weeks.

Couscous or Barley Cherry Tomato Salad

Recipe by: Sahar Usmani-Brown

2 cups barley or Israeli couscous cooked in chicken or vegetable stock

1 cup cherry tomatoes (1 small container if store-bought)

1 cup fresh basil chopped

1 tablespoon each of fresh parsley and fresh dill (optional)

1 cup roasted pine nuts

1 medium brick feta cheese

4 tablespoons olive oil

1½ lemons freshly squeezed

1. Cook the barley or Israeli couscous (whatever your pleasure; barley has more texture, and Israeli couscous is smoother) in either the chicken or vegetable stock until it is slightly al dente. Drain in a colander and allow it to cool.
2. Add the remaining ingredients, using the suggested proportions as a guide. Mix, toss, and serve.
3. For extra flair, add nasturtium flower buds or other edible flowers from your garden for garnish.

Gourmet Southern-Style Fried Green Tomatoes

> 2 medium-sized green tomatoes
> ¼ cup all-purpose flour
> ¼ cup yellow cornmeal
> 1 cup buttermilk
> 1 cup vegetable oil (we use ½ cup canola
>   and ½ cup olive oil)
> Garlic salt
> Sea salt
> Red pepper flakes
> Cayenne pepper

1. Slice the tomatoes into slices about ¼" (6mm) thick.
2. Combine all of the dry ingredients (that is everything except for the buttermilk and oil) in a shallow bowl, and pour the buttermilk into a second shallow bowl.
3. Heat the oil in a frying pan.
4. While the oil is heating, dip the green tomato slices in buttermilk and immediately coat both sides with the flour-and-cornmeal mixture.
5. Fry the dredged tomato slices for 3 to 5 minutes per side.

How to Roast Garlic

Roasted garlic is great to have on hand for delicious homemade garlic butter in a snap. Making it is so easy that you will wonder why you didn't try it sooner.

Start with a whole head of garlic and remove as much of the paper membrane from the outside as you can without separating the cloves. Place the garlic in a small glass baking dish with about ¼ cup of water, drizzle with about a tablespoon of olive oil, and cover the dish with a lid or foil. Bake in a preheated 375°F (190°C) oven for about 30 minutes. Remove it from the oven, baste with the oil-water mixture, and return to oven for another half hour or until the garlic is very soft. Refrigerate any leftovers in a sealed container for up to a week.

We recommend serving the tomatoes with both a balsamic reduction and hot sauce. A simple reduction can be made by simmering a basic balsamic vinaigrette over medium heat until it has reduced by half.

Make a green tomato stack with three slices of fried green tomato, a slice of fresh mozzarella, and a thick slice of country ham. Put it together like a sandwich and drizzle it with vinaigrette.

Casual Meals

Rosemary Lemon Chicken

> 1 whole roasting chicken
> 4 sprigs fresh rosemary
> 10 cloves garlic, peeled
> 2 lemons
> ¼ cup dry white wine, optional
> 4 tablespoons olive oil
> Sea salt to taste
> Fresh ground black pepper to taste

1. Preheat oven to 450°F (231°C).
2. Rub the chicken with 2 tablespoons of olive oil. Place 2 sprigs of rosemary and 6 cloves of peeled garlic into cavity.
3. Pull back the skin on the breast and insert one of the remaining sprigs of rosemary.
4. Place the remaining rosemary and garlic into the bottom of the roasting pan, along with the remaining olive oil.
5. Squeeze the juice of one lemon into the cavity of chicken and squeeze the remaining lemon over the chicken.
6. Pour the wine over the chicken if using, and sprinkle with salt and pepper to taste.
7. Turn the oven down to 325°F (162°C). Bake the chicken for 45 minutes, and then check to see if it is done.

Hummus Pizza

Recipe by: Sahar Usmani-Brown

> 1 thin crust store-bought pizza dough (Pillsbury refrigerated thin crust pizza dough works great)
> 1½ cups of hummus (about ½ of a large container of hummus)
> ½ medium red onion, cut into thin slices
> 1½ cups cherry tomatoes, sliced in half (about half a small container of store bought cherry tomatoes)
> 2 handfuls fresh basil
> Drizzle olive oil
> Light sprinkle paprika
> Sprinkle of cornmeal

Optional:

> Mushrooms
> Yellow or orange bell pepper
> Sage
> Thyme
> Red pepper flakes
> Fresh herbs from the garden

1. Preheat a pizza stone in a 425°F (217°C) oven (use a baking sheet in a pinch if you don't have a pizza stone, but a pizza stone improves the evenness of baking).
2. In a bowl, mix the red onion, cherry tomatoes, basil, and paprika in a bowl along with any other optional ingredients and drizzle lightly with olive oil.
3. Take heated stone out of the oven and sprinkle lightly with cornmeal to prevent sticking. On the counter, roll

Drying Your Fresh Herbs

Fresh herbs are a great thing to have on hand, but you will no doubt have plenty left over even after you've used them in all of your favorite recipes. Why not dry them so you have your very own home-grown herb collection all year round? If you have access to a food dehydrator, that is the preferred method. It's simple, requires very little attention, and you can't really do it wrong. If you need another way, try the oven method.

Set your oven to the lowest heat setting. Arrange your fresh herbs on a dry cookie sheet or baking dish and place it in the oven. Every hour or so, arrange the herbs to ensure that they are drying out evenly. When herbs are completely dry, they can be stored in an airtight container for several months, giving you plenty of time to use them before the next growing season yields more fresh herbs!

You can dry different herbs together at the same time as long as you keep them separate so they do not touch while they are drying out.

out the pizza dough with a rolling pin until thin and transfer the dough to the heated pizza stone. Spread hummus on the pizza dough and use the back of a spoon to evenly smooth it out.

4. Place the toppings mixture on the pizza. For added visual effect, if desired, line cherry tomatoes with the skin side down along the edges of the pizza dough. Drizzle lightly with olive oil and bake 25–35 minutes until the edges of the dough begin to brown. Cut and serve.

For an easy party treat, make multiple batches of premixed party spread, keep it in a refrigerator and assemble quick pizzas throughout the evening.

Greek Pasta Salad

> 1 pound penne pasta
> 1 green pepper, sliced into thin strips
> 2 ripe tomatoes, cubed
> ½ pound fresh baby spinach
> 1 cup kalamata olives
> 3 tablespoons pickled banana peppers
> 2 cups crumbled feta cheese
> ½ cup olive oil
> ½ cup red wine vinegar
> 4 cloves fresh garlic, crushed
> 2 teaspoons fresh oregano

½ teaspoon salt

Fresh ground black pepper to taste

1. Make the dressing by combining the garlic, oil, vinegar, salt, pepper, and fresh oregano in a small bowl and let it sit while you make the salad.
2. Cook the pasta until just tender and rinse it under cold water.
3. Mix the drained pasta and vegetables in a large bowl. Add the cheese and pour the dressing over all.
4. Serve chilled. This dish is best when allowed to sit for a couple of hours before serving.

Tabouli

3 cups finely chopped fresh parsley

½ cup finely chopped fresh mint leaves

2 green onions, chopped

3 cloves garlic, finely minced

4 or 5 fresh tomatoes, diced into small chunks

½ cup lemon juice

½ teaspoon allspice

½ teaspoon cumin

1 teaspoon salt

½ cup olive oil

Freshly ground black pepper to taste

1 cup bulgur wheat

2 cups boiling water

1. In a mixing bowl, pour the boiling water over the bulgur and allow it to stand as you prepare the vegetables.
2. Mix the chopped veggies herb and garlic together, and add the olive oil, lemon juice, and spices.
3. Drain and rinse the bulgur and mix it into the veggie mix.
4. Serve chilled on a bed of romaine lettuce, if desired.

Simple Stuffed Peppers

4 medium green bell peppers

1 pound lean ground beef

1 cup cooked white rice

1 cup purple onion, chopped

1 cup shredded cheddar or mozzarella cheese

2 cups tomatoes, crushed or pureed

1 teaspoon dried oregano

Salt to taste

Freshly ground black pepper to taste

Salsa (optional)

1. Preheat the oven or toaster oven to 375°F (190°C) and boil two quarts of water in a saucepan.
2. Remove the tops from bell peppers and remove the seeds. Drop the peppers into the pot of boiling water for 2 to 3 minutes, just until the color begins to turn a bright, vibrant green. Remove the peppers and allow them to cool.
3. Brown the ground beef and onions in a skillet over medium heat. Drain off the fat and return the beef and onions to the pan.
4. Add the rice, tomatoes, oregano, and cheese to the skillet and stir until well mixed. The mixture should be fairly thick.
5. Carefully spoon the mixture into each green pepper until it is completely full. Place the peppers in a small casserole dish. Sprinkle additional cheese and salsa (optional) on top of the peppers and bake for 20–25 minutes or until the tops begin to brown.

Michael's Summer Tomato Soup

4 large tomatoes

½ cup Vidalia onion (any mild, sweet variety will do), chopped

3 tablespoons olive oil

Fresh rosemary (an 8" [20cm] sprig)

1 tablespoon lemon zest, grated

A few leaves of fresh basil to taste

2 cups vegetable stock (or chicken stock)

Sea salt to taste

Freshly ground black pepper to taste

1. In a food processor, puree the tomatoes until smooth. I leave the peels on, but you can remove the seeds and peels to suit your taste.
2. Sauté the onions and fresh rosemary in olive oil over medium heat, approximately 8–10 minutes or until translucent.
3. Lower the heat, add the lemon zest and tomato puree to the onions and simmer for 15–20 minutes.
4. Add the stock and basil and simmer for another 15–20 minutes.

This is a simple and absolutely delicious soup that I actually enjoy chilled (which would technically make it a gazpacho) for a cool lunch just as much as I love to serve it with some crusty homemade bread for dinner. It's light and flavorful.

To be honest, I've omitted a few of my favorite ingredients because everyone always tells me that I make it too spicy. If you have a cast iron stomach like I do, feel free to replace the black pepper with cayenne and add some fresh chopped peppers to the finished product. If you like heat, you'll love it in this soup!

Salad Niçoise

2 boiled eggs

2 boiled new potatoes

10 cherry tomatoes

20 pitted olives (black or green)

Baby lettuce

7 oz. cooked green beans

2 tablespoons olive oil

1 lemon

Salt to taste

Freshly ground black pepper to taste

1. Quarter the eggs, potatoes, and tomatoes.
2. Combine the tomatoes, eggs, olives, and potatoes in a large bowl with the lettuce and green beans.
3. Add the olive oil and a squeeze of the lemon to the other ingredients.
4. Season with salt and pepper and serve.

Sage Marinated Chicken

4 cloves fresh garlic, chopped

½ cup fresh sage leaves

Juice from 4 lemons

1 cup white wine

1 dash hot sauce

1 teaspoon salt

½ teaspoon freshly ground black pepper

⅓ cup olive oil

Whole chicken, cleaned

1. Combine all the ingredients and marinate a whole, clean chicken in the marinade. Leave in the refrigerator at least 4 hours, preferably overnight.

2. Preheat the oven to 450°F (231°C). Drain the marinade, reserving the garlic and a few sage leaves. Stuff the sage and garlic into the cavity of the chicken.
3. Place the chicken in the preheated oven, turning the heat down to 325°F (162°C).
4. Bake until the chicken is tender, about 1 hour.

Ed's Squash Soup

6 tablespoons extra virgin olive oil

3 medium onions, chopped

2 butternut squash, halved and roasted

1 head garlic, roasted

2–3 teaspoons grated fresh ginger

2 potatoes, peeled and cut up

2 carrots, peeled and sliced thin

8 cups vegetable or chicken stock

Salt to taste

Freshly ground black pepper to taste

A few sprigs of fresh parsley, chopped

1½ teaspoon dried thyme leaves, crumbled

1 or 2 cups cream, milk or half-and-half

1. Pour the olive oil into the large soup pot and slowly cook onions over medium-low heat until lightly browned.
2. Add roasted squash and roasted garlic, ginger, potatoes, and carrots. Pour in the stock, stir well, and bring to a boil. Reduce the heat, cover, and simmer for 45 minutes.
3. Add the seasonings and parsley and simmer for another 15 minutes. Cool, add the cream, and blend in batches in a blender or food processor.
4. Reheat the soup in a clean pot and serve with fresh thyme as a garnish.

Casual Extras

White Tomato Sorbet

Though it may seem like it, this isn't a dessert dish. It is a great cold complement to shrimp or crab dishes in those sultry summer months! It's best used with cherry tomatoes, but you can use other varieties if you want (it just makes it a little pinker).

   2 pounds cherry tomatoes

   1 cup water

   $2/3$ cup sugar

   $1/8$ oz (¾ teaspoon) gelatin

1. Wash the cherry tomatoes and place them whole through a juicing machine, collecting the liquid in a pan.
2. Heat the tomato liquid, and as soon as it's about to boil, take it off the heat and pass it through a sieve or cloth. (Do not let it boil.)
3. Boil the sugar and water together. Add the gelatin and stir until blended.
4. Mix the sugar water with the clear tomato liquid.
5. Allow the mixture to cool slightly, then place it into an ice-cream machine until it is hard. If you do not have an ice-cream machine, simply place the mixture in the freezer, stirring it every hour until it is set.

Need a little something extra to make your meal pop? Give one of these recipes a try!

Green Tomato Chutney

   2 pounds green tomatoes

   Large pinch poppy seeds

   Half an onion

   1 garlic clove

   2½ tablespoons white wine vinegar

   Thyme and bay leaves

   Pinch of salt and pepper

   ½ cup sugar

1. Cut the tomatoes into small pieces and finely chop the onion and garlic.
2. Place all the ingredients together in a pan with about a ½ cup of water and cook for about 1 hour.
3. After all the ingredients have cooked down or reached the correct consistency, allow the chutney to cool and then taste it for seasoning.
4. Place the chutney in a jar and store refrigerated for up to two weeks.

Tomato Butter

This recipe is a great way to spice up any steak and give that something extra to anything grilled or barbecued.

   6 tomatoes, halved and deseeded

   3 sprigs thyme, leaves only

   2 tablespoons olive oil

   2 sticks of butter, softened

   Salt to taste

   Freshly ground black pepper to taste

1. Preheat the oven to 425°F (217°C). Place the tomatoes on a baking sheet, cut side up, and season with salt and pepper.
2. Sprinkle the tomatoes with thyme leaves and drizzle the olive oil over them.

3. Place the tomatoes in the oven and roast for 20 minutes. Turn off the oven and leave the tomatoes in the oven for 4–5 hours, or overnight, until they are semi-dried but still soft.
4. Allow the butter to soften and add the roasted tomatoes.
5. Pulse in a blender until combined.
6. Check the seasoning and add more salt and pepper if necessary.
7. Spoon the tomato butter along a piece of cling film.
8. Wrap the cling film around the butter and roll it up tightly to form a sausage shape, twisting the film at both ends to seal.
9. Place the butter in the refrigerator for at least an hour, until it is chilled and firm.

When the butter is hard, slice it into the desired thickness and place it on top of a freshly cooked steak.

Zucchini Cranberry Muffins

2½ cups all-purpose flour

1 cup sugar

2½ teaspoons baking powder

½ teaspoon baking soda

1 teaspoon ground cinnamon

1 teaspoon ground nutmeg

½ teaspoon salt

½ cup butter or margarine

¼ cup milk

Juice from 1 lemon

1 teaspoon grated lemon zest

2 eggs, lightly beaten

1½ cups shredded zucchini

1 teaspoon vanilla extract

1 cup dried cranberries

1. Preheat the oven to 350°F (176°C).
2. Mix the milk and lemon juice and set aside.
3. Cream together the butter, sugar, eggs, and vanilla. Stir in the zucchini and lemon zest.
4. Combine the remaining dry ingredients in a separate bowl and gradually add them to the wet ingredients.
5. Add the milk/lemon juice and mix thoroughly.
6. Carefully fold in the cranberries.
7. Spray a cupcake tin with nonstick cooking spray or use cupcake liners and fill each one about ⅔ full.
8. Bake at 350°F (176°C) for 15 minutes or until the muffins are lightly browned on top.

Sage in Browned Butter

½ cup fresh sage leaves (Note: This will not work with dried sage.)

1 cup fresh butter

1 clove garlic, minced

2 tablespoons minced fresh parsley

Freshly ground black pepper to taste

1. Heat the butter over medium heat. Cut the sage leaves into strips and add them to the pan when the butter is melted.
2. Sauté slowly until the butter looks a bit browned around the edges and the sage is very fragrant. Make sure not to burn the sage.
3. Just before you remove the pan from the heat, add the minced garlic and stir. Remove from the heat and add minced parsley and some pepper.

This is a wonderful finish to pasta or chicken. It is also a great accompaniment to gnocchi, and makes a yummy bread dip with an antipasto plate.

8 Casual Connections

The information in this book is only a starting point on your urban gardening journey. In this chapter, you'll find lots of great resources for everything from supplies, tools, and plants to inspiration and community. Of course, these are just suggestions. Feel free to try any brand of tool or seeds and seek out your own community. You never know what you will find.

We've also included a bit more information about the folks you read about throughout the book. Think of it as a behind-the-scenes peek.

Garden Evaluation Worksheet

SCALE: 1 square = 1 square foot

Using the grid at the left, sketch out your garden area, including any buildings, sidewalks, and other permanent fixtures.

You can adjust the scale as needed for the size of your available space. Attaching a photo of your space can be a big help if you take your worksheet to a local garden center for advice. Answer the following questions to get a complete picture of what you are working with:

Sun
Full / Partial / Shade
Notes: _____
_____
_____
_____
_____
_____
_____
_____

Traffic
Heavy/Moderate/Low
Notes: _____
_____
_____
_____
_____
_____
_____
_____
_____

Wind
Heavy/Moderate/Low
Notes: _____
_____
_____
_____
_____
_____
_____
_____
_____

Add notes about any other specific challenges or design ideas you have, as well as plants you would like to grow.
_____
_____
_____
_____
_____
_____
_____
_____
_____
_____
_____
_____
_____
_____
_____

Seeds, Plants, Tools, and Supplies

Ames True Temper

www.ames.com

A leading manufacturer of non-powered garden equipment and tools throughout North America, including the brands Ames, True Temper, Union Tools, Jackson Professional. and Razor-Back.

Annie's Annuals

www.anniesannuals.com

Located in Richmond, California, Annie's Annuals has created a name for itself over the course of more than twenty years in business. From its humble beginnings as the backyard hobby of founder and owner Annie Hayes to the 2½ acre nursery that now serves dozens of independent retail centers, Annie's Annuals is proud of its reputation and proud to offer mail-order services to those outside of their geographic area.

Burpee Seeds

www.burpee.com

What can you say about a seed company that's been in business since 1876 and is still going strong? You can say that Burpee still has some of the highest-quality seeds, plants, and garden products in North America! Whether you opt for mail order or you find Burpee products in your local retailer, you can be sure that a Burpee product is among the best in the world.

Fiskars

www.fiskars.com

Fiskars makes a slew of thoughtfully designed gardening products. From barrels to collect rain water to engine-free reel mowers, these gadgets are sure to please.

Seed Savers Exchange

www.seedsavers.org

Founded in 1975 by Dianne Ott Whealy and Kent Whealy as a way of preserving the heritage and history of heirloom seeds, Seed Savers Exchange now boasts the largest non-government seed library in the United States with more than 25,000 seed varieties in the library.

From the SSE website: *"Seed Savers Exchange is a nonprofit, member-supported organization that saves and shares the heirloom seeds of our garden heritage, forming a living legacy that can be passed down through generations."*

Tomato Bob

www.tomatobob.com

Have you ever heard of a Costoluto Genovese or a White Wonder heirloom tomato? Tomato Bob has! What can we say about Tomato Bob? Bob and his family carry more than seven hundred different varieties of heirloom tomato, pepper, veggie, herb, and flower seeds, many of which have been handed down through generations, the way seeds have been throughout history. Tomato Bob's customer service is nothing short of top shelf, and the company offers a 100 percent guarantee on every seed it sells. It's been in business for more than ten years, and it is no wonder why.

Free and Low-Cost Gardening Supplies

From UrbanGardenCasual.com.

Helping people save money while gardening is something we're passionate about. One area where these two world converge is in resources that are the perfect hunting grounds for free and low-cost gardening supplies. Here are two of our favorites:

Craigslist is the site responsible for making classified ads cool. There are Craigslist mini websites for major cities in every state. Each of these sites contains user-generated classified ads for everything from personal ads to real estate listings.

The areas of Craigslist that have the most value to urban gardeners include Barter and Farm + Garden under the For Sale heading, and Farm + Garden under the Services heading. You can find everything from heirloom seedlings to 55 gallon drums for next to nothing, and each interaction makes the gardening world just a little bit smaller.

More at www.craigslist.org.

Freecycle is a movement and a network of nearly five thousand grassroots groups with millions of members worldwide whose sole purpose is to give things away. When you join your local Freecycle group (and chances are really good that you will have one close to you), you will be greeted with an e-mail that explains the etiquette and protocol for that particular list as well as any specific instructions.

Generally speaking, the lists work the same way: You have a box of something that you no longer need, but you don't want to toss it in the garbage and clog the landfill with the useless stuff you bought on a whim at 3 A.M. from the shopping channel. You send a message to the Freecycle list telling everyone what you have, and people can then respond telling you they want the items you're offering. Our readers have been lucky enough to find everything from a truckload of reclaimed cedar barn wood (that became raised beds) to a collection of more than two dozen packets of heirloom tomato seeds, some of which had been passed down through generations.

More at www.freecycle.org.

One of the best ways to save money on gardening supplies is to share the expense with others. Most folks in an urban environment don't need an entire packet of seeds. By forming a mini co-op with other urban gardeners, you can purchase a good selection of seed varieties and then divide them among the participants.

The same rules can apply to gardening equipment that you might not need every day. Make purchases with others and then share the use of your supplies on an as-needed basis. Not only does this save you quite a bit of money, it also encourages you to interact and socialize with like-minded people in your neighborhood, and that is what gardening is all about.

Victory Seeds

www.victoryseeds.com

By keeping close to its original ideals of preserving heirloom seeds and their historic importance, the Victory Seed Company has been able to remain a small, family-owned and -operated company that practices what it preaches by growing its own seeds and supporting seed farming by purchasing from authorized growers that share its dedication to historic preservation.

Events, Publications, and Media

Farmer's Almanac

www.almanac.com

The longest continuously published periodical in North America, *The Farmer's Almanac* is the one thing we recommend that everyone should own. From tide tables to sunrise and planting charts, even weather forecasts (that are far more accurate than anything you'll get on the six o'clock news) and recipes, this must-have annual magazine has been around since 1792 and will outlive us all.

By Phone: 800-223-3166

By Mail: The Old Farmer's Almanac

P.O. Box 422453, Palm Coast, FL 32142-2453

Garden Girl TV

www.gardengirltv.com

Patti Moreno has more charm and personality than most of us combined, and it has helped to make her one of the most popular garden personalities in America. As a contributor to *Fine Gardening, Organic Gardening Magazine,* and *The Farmer's Almanac,* you can trust that her charm is only matched by her gardening knowledge!

Go Green Expo

www.gogreenexpo.com

This company hosts a series of eco-friendly green business-to-business and business-to-consumer events across the country.

Growing a Greener World

www.growingagreenerworld.com

This groundbreaking PBS series brings the gardening message to a new, modern audience. Hosted by two of the most recognized names in garden media, Joe Lamp'l and Patti Moreno, *Growing a Greener World* combines time-honored, traditional gardening techniques with a fresh and eco-friendly message. The pair creates an interactive experience like no other by inviting the audience to play a part through social media outlets like Twitter and Facebook. Celebrity chef Nathan Lyon joins the team as well.

Mother Earth News

www.motherearthnews.com.

Mother Earth News is a popular sustainable lifestyle magazine that provides expert coverage on organic foods and greener living.

Blogs and Informational Websites

American Community Garden Association

www.communitygarden.org

This organization's mission is to strengthen communities by strengthening community gardens. Throughout the United States and Canada, the American Community Garden Association works as a binational organization of gardening aficionados from all walks of life who are striving to improve quality of life, stimulate social interaction, spur self-reliant behavior, produce healthy food, lower food costs, and conserve resources.

City Farmer's Urban Agriculture Notes

www.cityfarmer.info and www.cityfarmer.org
A treasure trove of information, this Canadian organization has been around since 1978, and its message has been consistent since then—urban people need to grow something edible!

Dave's Garden

www.davesgarden.com
An informational website for garden folk around the world, Dave's Garden is one of the most educational resources on the Web today. For more than a decade, this site has housed a growing database of tools for gardeners, by gardeners.

Garden Guides

www.gardenguides.com
Garden Guides sets its goals pretty high. It aims to be the "best online resource for gardening enthusiasts," and with the sheer volume of plant info sheets, guides, tips, techniques, and recipes on the website, it is obviously a goal it takes very seriously.

Homegrown.org

http://homegrown.org
Created by Farm Aid, Homegrown.org is an online community that seeks to celebrate people who eat, grow, and cook good food. Member groups, blogs, and discussion boards make interaction both fun and informative. Info on DIY projects, growing food, preparing food, and even music and art can be found here.

Insects @ About.com

http://insects.about.com
Writer and photographer Debbie Hadley has spent more than fifteen years as a dedicated naturalist and educator. If you have specific questions about insects in your garden, Debbie is the person to ask.

Life on the Balcony

www.lifeonthebalcony.com
Sunset Magazine refers to Fern Richardson's Life on the Balcony blog thusly: "This love poem to container gardening and planting in tiny spaces proves that no bare earth is no excuse not to garden." We couldn't have said it better. Fern is a virtual force to be reckoned with, and she also has a really cool name (that she swears was given to her at birth).

Organic Gardening @ About.com

http://organicgardening.about.com
Hosted by expert site guide Colleen Vanderlinden, Organic Gardening @ About.com is a feature-filled resource with tons of fantastic information on every aspect of organic gardening from starting a garden to weeds, diseases, and pest control. Colleen is co-author of the book *Edible Gardening for the Midwest*.

Our Friend Ben

http://ourfriendben.wordpress.com
Our Friend Ben is the online *nom de plume* for an author, editor, and homesteader in Pennsylvania who has been

a friend of the Urban Garden Casual family for years. Ben's blog reads like a lush piece of literature with events unfolding in such a way that will leave you begging for the next installment.

Plant Whatever Brings You Joy

www.plantwhateverbringsyoujoy.com
Internationally known book publicist Kathryn Hall has a way with words and a way with plants. Her blog combines these talents with her keen eye for nature photography.

Red, White and Grew

http://redwhiteandgrew.com
In a society where nearly anything can be seen as politically polarizing, writer Pamela Price has created a blog that "promotes the victory garden revival and other simple, earth-friendly endeavors as bipartisan, patriotic acts in an age of uncertainty." The well-written and researched content is easy to read and informative.

Tomato Casual

www.tomatocasual.com
As the first sister site to Urban Garden Casual, Tomato Casual takes the casual philosophy to the extreme and feeds the needs of a very special and growing segment of the population—the few, the proud, the tomato obsessed. As the first website of its kind to be dedicated to "Everything Tomato for People Who Love Tomatoes," Tomato Casual runs the gamut from growing, eating, and cooking with tomatoes to music, art, and even movies and books that feature our favorite fruit.

Urban Garden Casual

www.urbangardencasual.com
Founded in the summer of 2007, Urban Garden Casual grew from its humble roots as the brainchild of Reggie Solomon's decidedly casual ideas into an online center helping city dwellers to reclaim the pleasures of noncity living within the confines of urban space. Bridging traditional gardening with the special needs of urban and small-space gardeners in the modern world, Urban Garden Casual encourages people worldwide to shed their work clothes, pick up their iPods, and embark on a journey through the world of gardening done urban and gardening done casual.

The Urban Garden Project

www.urbangardenproject.com
What happens when two inexperienced guys decide to give urban gardening a shot for the first time? Ben Fairfield and Jared Lyda sought to answer that question when they created The Urban Garden Project in Northern Idaho. The website features a lot of hands-on DIY instructional videos and other great information presented in an easy-to-read format.

United States Department of Agriculture

www.usda.gov
The official online presence of the USDA houses more information than most of us could ever hope to learn on everything from agriculture to law, food, and nutrition to natural resources and the environment. If this site isn't in your bookmarked list yet, it should be.

Books

There is just not much better in life than curling up with a good book. Here are a few suggestions from the Urban Garden Casual team for books that are great for urban gardeners and the people who love us:

Square Foot Gardening by Mel Bartholemew. This book might well be considered the bible for small-space gardening. Mel Bartholemew first presented his method for laying out your vegetable gardens in square foot increments in 1981 in the original printing of this book, and it has been a nonstop favorite ever since. Mel's plan was so popular that it led to a PBS series on the subject. The Urban Garden Casual team is a fan of the square foot method, and the results are plain to see for anyone who has ever tried it. You will have a more-compact, better-producing garden with less effort than you ever imagined possible. A win-win situation indeed!

Garden Wizardry for Kids by L. Patricia Kite and *Roots, Shoots, Buckets & Boots: Gardening Together with Children* by Sharon Lovejoy. Everyone with a love for gardening and the outdoors longs for ways to include their children in their pursuits. These books are perfect ways to do just that. Each describes experiments and ideas for helping your children gain a love of gardening, and they do so in fun and imaginative ways such as planting a "Pizza Patch" and even growing your own peanuts! You will be giddy with the possibilities presented and eager to learn in your urban garden space with your children right by your side.

(Above) Photo by Ric Deliantoni.

McGee & Stuckey's Bountiful Container: Create Container Gardens of Vegetables, Herbs, Fruits, and Edible Flowers by Rose Marie Nichols McGee and Maggie Stuckey. As you've seen throughout our book, containers are the perfect answer for those who might not have a lot of space or a traditional garden plot upon which to plant. This book is four hundred pages describing the many plants that will thrive in a container. There are also theme gardens suggested, and many tips and techniques for getting the most out of your container garden.

Don't Throw It, Grow It! by Deborah Peterson and Millicent Selsam. The authors show the methods used to grow new plants from sixty-eight different fruits, nuts, herbs, and spices, and even include a few we had never heard of! Fancy a malanga or genip?

Apps

Just a few short years ago, some of us were still using rotary telephones at home, and now standard home telephone service is a relic of days gone by, replaced by smart phones that are able to keep us in touch by phone, text message, e-mail, and instant messaging. There are even special applications, or *apps,* that make your iPhone do just about anything you could possibly imagine. Search for these gardening apps on iTunes by typing the name of the app into the search field.

iLocate - Gardening Supplies

by Arctic Gerbil Creations is a cool app that makes easy work of finding the nearest gardening supplies retailer based on your GPS location.

iGarden USA - Gardening Helper

by NanoSoft, LLC covers a variety of vegetables, herbs and fruits along with planting dates based on your hardiness zone. The app allows you to incorporate your own seeds along with planting information and photos.

Landscaper's Companion

by Stevenson Software, LLC contains info on well over 1,400 plants in sixteen categories. Nearly 6,000 photographs make it a visually useful garden plant guide that you will want to have in your mobile arsenal.

Miscellaneous Resources

Grow Your Own Greens With Salad Tables & Salad Boxes

www.hgic.umd.edu/_media/documents/hg601.pdf
We talked about salad tables in chapter 5. This is a fantastic printable step-by-step guide to building your own salad table complete with materials list, illustrated instructions, and alternative building methods.

P-Patch (Seattle, Washington)

www.seattle.gov/neighborhoods/ppatch
The P-Patch, so named for the Picardo family who gave it its beginnings in the early 1970s, is one of the largest groups of community gardens in the world with more than seventy-five separate gardens within the collective and a waiting list for new gardeners. The P-Patch Trust is a not-for-profit organization that manages the gardens in conjunction with the Seattle Department of Neighborhoods. The community gardens of P-Patch are 100 percent organic.

DIY Self-Watering Container

http://rooftopgardens.ca/files/manual 2009 web.pdf
This eight-page printable file is easily one of the most detailed and easy-to-understand step-by-step guides to building your own self-watering container using easily accessible materials that are quite inexpensive.

The Windowfarms Project

www.windowfarms.org
The biggest challenge of gardening in an urban environment has to be a lack of available and usable space. One grassroots organization in New York City has come up with a way to ensure that nearly everyone can grow something, and support for this group's interesting concept is growing.

The Windowfarms Project may seem a bit farfetched at first, but the simple idea makes perfect sense when you look just a little deeper. According to the website, their goal is to ultimately see a "shift in attitudes toward the green revolution." Created by a pair of artists named Britta Riley and Rebecca Bray in early 2009, the project had the support of the Eyebeam Art and Technology Center, as well as a sponsorship from the pair's design firm.

The idea centers around using the abundance of available window space in urban cities and beyond as vertical farming space, enabling city dwellers to grow their own herbs, veggies, and fruit in hydroponic window gardens that they can construct themselves. The plans are very easy to follow and can be downloaded at no cost from the Windowfarms website.

Not yet convinced that the idea will fly? Consider this fact: The first Windowfarms prototype system held twenty-five plants and grew a salad a week during the winter months in a 4' × 6' (1.2m × 1.8m) window with dim light. The plans call for the use of inexpensive items that are either readily available at any local hardware store or make use of recycled materials.

The Windowfarms Project is focused not only on growing food but also on the innovation that can come about as a result of crowdsourcing. The group encourages people to perfect and add to their designs, showing that regular people can indeed play an active and important role in the "green revolution." This process, called R&D-I-Y (short for Research and Develop It Yourself), is a new answer to standard industry research-and-development practices that are often limiting and unable or unwilling to take advantage of the consumer's ability to make innovative changes.

Profiles in Casual

The people we selected for the Profiles in Casual segments featured in each chapter were chosen because they are excellent examples of what is being accomplished by urban gardeners across the country. They are a diverse group of people that we are proud to count among our friends.

Chapter 2: Ivette Soler

www.thegerminatrix.com
Ivette Soler has the uncanny ability to translate her infectious personality into the garden spaces she creates. Whether creating a bold outdoor statement for some of the biggest names in entertainment or working within the confines of the smallest of private courtyard gardens, she infuses her work with the unapologetic approach of a true artist.

Chapter 3: Mike Lieberman

www.urbanorganicgardener.com

Born and raised in the Canarsie neighborhood of Brooklyn, New York, Mike Lieberman is as unique and diverse as the world in which we live. An advocate of simple living that is in line with environmental principles and a healthy lifestyle, Mike writes and speaks on topics ranging from urban gardening to sustainability, recycling to raw food recipes. In his own words, "My goal is to teach you to tear down all the fluff and to provide you some simple solutions for living in this world made complex."

Chapter 4: Shala and James Cross

www.doubledanger.com

This Texas duo definitely packs a double punch. Not only are they truly obsessed with gardening (our favorite type of people), but their website splits its time between their copious garden pursuits and James's obsession with the perfect barbecue and bacon. In their own words, "mix equal parts gardening and BBQ and stir lazily." Indeed, my friends. Indeed.

Chapter 5: Meg Graustein

Meg Graustein is a New Haven, Connecticut, native with a green thumb and passion for urban gardening and living a sustainable, eco-friendly lifestyle. When she is not tending her own garden, she serves as the Green Job Corps Program manager for the New Haven Ecology Project, home to Common Ground High School, a nonprofit urban farm and environmental education center in New Haven, Connecticut.

Chapter 6: Joe Lamp'l, a.k.a. joe gardener

www.joegardener.com

Joe Lamp'l is a busy man. An avid gardener for more than thirty years, Joe is also the author of several books, including *The Green Gardener's Guide*. Not one to rest on a job well done, he is also the nationally recognized television host of *Fresh from the Garden* on the DIY Network, *GardenSMART* and *Growing a Greener World* on PBS, as well as being the spokesperson for the Fiskars Project Orange Thumb program. There is no denying that when Joe tells you that he is dedicated to "growing a greener world,"™ he really means it!

Chapter 7: The Shibaguyz

www.shibaguyz.com

Shannon and Jason Mullet-Bowlsby are more than just urban gardeners; they are an undeniable force to be reckoned with in nearly every aspect of their life. From gardening both at home and in community gardens across Seattle, Washington, to canning and giving lessons on food preservation, you'd think the pair would have enough on their plate, but you would miss their fondness for their ever-growing Shiba Inu family and their affinity for spinning their own fibers by hand. Renaissance men if ever there were such a thing, Shannon and Jason are a fine example of what you can accomplish with dedication, drive, and just a little dose of insanity.

Authors and Contributors

Reggie Solomon: Author

A native of South Georgia, T. Reginald Solomon (Reggie, please) came about his love for gardening honestly. Both of Reggie's parents, Elbert and Thelma, were themselves born into farming families in Mississippi, leading him to eventually discover what he now considers his modern farming legacy—urban gardening.

Reggie took that legacy to heart and created the websites UrbanGardenCasual.com and TomatoCasual.com, sites from which the origins of this book are found. He is an alumnus of Yale College and the Harvard Kennedy School. Reggie works at Yale University and lives in New Haven, Connecticut, where he likes to go wine-tasting and hip-hop dancing with friends in his free time.

Michael Nolan: Author

A lifelong casual-lifestyle gardener of more than thirty years, Michael Nolan is the founder of the Riverside Community Garden in Atlanta, Georgia. The aptly named "garden rock star" has an admittedly unconventional approach to life that carries over into his gardening. In true rock-star style, Michael challenges conventions by growing tomato and pepper plants indoors during the winter months. He also eats dandelion greens, raw.

When he isn't gardening, Michael spends much of his time working to raise money and awareness for breast cancer. He walks in the Susan G. Komen Breast Cancer 3-Day for the Cure, runs in the Race for the Cure and is a founding member of The 2nd Basemen, a fraternal organization of men and women devoted to stopping breast cancer.

Vanessa Richins: Contributor

Vanessa Richins is a garden educator and writer who grew up amid the lush palms and eucalyptus trees of Southern California and now calls Utah, with its linens and maples, home. Her bachelor's degree in horticulture (she started out in microbiology) from Brigham Young University served to feed her lifelong love of plants. Vanessa serves as the About.com Guide for Trees and Shrubs, and she teaches gardening and topiary classes in the Utah Valley University community education program. She is a long time writer for both UrbanGardenCasual.com and TomatoCasual.com.

Michelle Fabio: Contributor

An American-born resident of Calabria in beautiful southern Italy, Michelle Fabio's *curriculum vitae* is nearly as impressive as her love for gardening. She works as a freelance writer, translator, and attorney (yes, really).

Michelle's blog is as colorful and entertaining as she is. Read it at http://bleedingespresso.com.

Chris McLaughlin: Contributor

www.asuburbanfarmer.com

The author of *The Complete Idiot's Guide to Composting* and *The Complete Idiot's Guide to Growing Heirloom Vegetables*, Chris McLaughlin is a composting guru and true suburban farmer with a love for plants and animals that include worms, rabbits, and horses, all of which she keeps.

Index

(Above) Photo by Ric Deliantoni.

Books of Interest

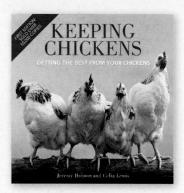

Keeping Chickens

Chickens can be the perfect addition to your garden. They consume weeds and can provide you with a natural food source. This book shows you exactly how to care for a small flock by covering everything from choosing the right breed to feeding and housing. Plus you'll find fun egg recipes, feather-and-egg craft projects, and even a look at how chickens interact with children and other pets. ISBN-13: 978-0-7153-3625-0; ISBN-10: 0-7153-3625-8, paperback, 176 pages, #Z7135

Living Large on Less

You don't have to be a financial whiz (or even mathematically inclined) to manage your money. *Living Large on Less* is full of hundreds of ways to save money without drastically altering your lifestyle. You can eat the food you want, wear your favorite designer's clothes, take a dream vacation, and throw a great party without breaking the bank. With this advice, you'll never pay full-price again. ISBN-13: 978-1-4403-0432-3; ISBN-10: 1-4403-0432-7, paperback, 224 pages, #Z7133

Organized Simplicity

Simplicity isn't about what you give up. It's about what you gain. When you remove the things that don't matter to you, you are free to focus on only the things that are meaningful to you. Imagine your home, your time, your finances, and your belongings all filling you with positive energy and helping you achieve your dreams. It can happen, and *Organized Simplicity* can show you how. ISBN-13: 978-1-4403-0263-3; ISBN-10: 1-4403-0263-4, hardcover with concealed spiral, 256 pages, #Z6515

These books and other fine Betterway Home titles are available at your local bookstore and from online suppliers. Visit our website at www.betterwaybooks.com.